The GCSE: an uncommon examination

Bedford Way Papers

ISSN 0261—0078

1. 'Fifteen Thousand Hours': A Discussion
Barbara Tizard et al.
ISBN 0 85473 090 7

3. Issues in Music Education
Charles Plummeridge et al.
ISBN 0 85473 105 9

4. No Minister: A Critique of the D E S Paper 'The School Curriculum'
John White et al.
ISBN 0 85473 115 6

5. Publishing School Examination Results: A Discussion
Ian Plewis et al.
ISBN 0 85473 116 4

8. Girls and Mathematics: The Early Years
Rosie Walden and Valerie Walkerdine
ISBN 0 85473 124 5

9. Reorganisation of Secondary Education in Manchester
Dudley Fiske
ISBN 0 85473 125 3

11. The Language Monitors
Harold Rosen
ISBN 0 85473 134 2

12. Meeting Special Educational Needs: The 1981 Act and its Implications
John Welton et al.
ISBN 0 85473 136 9

13. Geography in Education Now
Norman Graves et al.
ISBN 0 85473 219 5

14. Art and Design Education: Heritage and Prospect
Anthony Dyson et al.
ISBN 0 85473 245 4

15. Is Teaching a Profession?
Peter Gordon (ed.)
ISBN 0 85473 220 9

16. Teaching Political Literacy
Alex Porter (ed.)
ISBN 0 85473 154 7

17. Opening Moves: Study of Children's Language Development
Margaret Meek (ed.)
ISBN 0 85473 161 X

18. Secondary School Examinations
Jo Mortimore, Peter Mortimore and Clyde Chitty
ISBN 0 85473 259 4

19. Lessons Before Midnight: Educating for Reason in Nuclear Matters
The Bishop of Salisbury, et al
ISBN 0 85473 189 X

20. Education plc?: Headteachers and the New Training Initiative
Janet Maw et al
ISBN 0 85473 191 1

21. The Tightening Grip: Growth of Central Control of the School Curriculum
Denis Lawton
ISBN 0 85473 201 2

22. The Quality Controllers: A Critique of the White Paper 'Teaching Quality'
Frances Slater (ed.)
ISBN 0 85473 212 8

23. Education: Time for a New Act?
Richard Aldrich and Patricia Leighton
ISBN 0 85473 217 9

24. Girls and Mathematics: from Primary to Secondary Schooling
Rosie Walden and Valerie Walkerdine
ISBN 0 85473 222 5

25. Psychology and Schooling: What's the Matter?
Guy Claxton et al.
ISBN 0 85473 228 4

26. Sarah's Letters: A Case of Shyness
Bernard T Harrison
ISBN 0 85473 241 1

27 The Infant School: past, present and future
Rosemary Davis (ed.)
ISBN 0 85473 250 0

28 The Politics of Health Information
Wendy Farrant and Jill Russell
ISBN 0 85473 260 8

29 The GCSE: an uncommon examination
Caroline Gipps (ed.)
ISBN 0 85473 262 4

30 Education for a Pluralist Society
Graham Haydon (ed.)
ISBN 0 85473 263 2

31 Lessons in Partnership: an INSET course as a case study
Elizabeth Cowne & Brahm Norwich
ISBN 0 85473 267 5

32. Redefining the Comprehensive Experience
Clyde Chitty (ed.)
ISBN 0 85473 280 2

33. The National Curriculum
Denis Lawton and Clyde Chitty (eds.)
ISBN 0 85473 294 2

The GCSE
an uncommon examination

Caroline Gipps (ed.), Henry Macintosh,
Harry Torrance, Roger Murphy,
Harvey Goldstein and Desmond Nuttall

Bedford Way Papers 29
Institute of Education, University of London
distributed by Turnaround Distribution Ltd

First published in 1986 by the Institute of Education, University of London,
20 Bedford Way, London WC1H 0AL. Reprinted 1988.

Distributed by Turnaround Distribution Ltd., 27 Horsell Road,
London N5 1XL (telephone: 01-609 7836).

The opinions expressed in these papers are those of the authors and do not necessarily reflect those of the publisher.

© Institute of Education, University of London, 1986
All rights reserved.

ISBN 0 85473 262 4

British Library Cataloguing in Publication Data

The GCSE an uncommon examination. — (Bedford Way papers, ISSN 0261-0078; 29)
  1. General Certificate of Secondary Education
  I. Gipps, Caroline   II. Series
  373.12'62   LB3056.G7

ISBN 0-85473-262-4

Printed in Great Britain by Reprographic Services
Institute of Education, University of London.
Typesetting by Joan Rose

153/154-001-066-1186

Contents

	Page
Notes on Contributors	7
Preface *Caroline Gipps*	9
GCSE: some background *Caroline Gipps*	11
The Sacred Cows of Coursework *Henry Macintosh*	21
School-based Assessment in GCSE: aspirations, problems and possibilities *Harry Torrance*	30
The Emperor Has No Clothes: grade criteria and the GCSE *Roger Murphy*	43
Can Graded Assessments, Records of Achievement and Modular Assessment Co-exist with GCSE? *Harvey Goldstein and Desmond Nuttall*	55

Notes on Contributors

Caroline Gipps is Lecturer in Curriculum Studies at the Institute of Education, University of London. She has been involved in research into the impact of LEA testing programmes, the work of the Assessment of Performance Unit and the role of testing in the identification of children with special needs. Earlier in her career she was involved in test development.

Harvey Goldstein is Professor of Statistical Methods at the Institute of Education, University of London. He has researched a number of issues related to the theory of assessment and testing, the application of statistical models to education systems, and the design and analysis of longitudinal studies.

Herny Macintosh was until recently Secretary to the Southern Regional Examinations Board and is now consultant for the TVEI Unit on Assessment and Accreditation based at the University of Surrey. He has for many years been involved in the International Association for Educational Assessment and has written a number of important texts for teachers on assessment.

Roger Murphy is Director of the Assessment and Examinations Unit at the University of Southampton which has a range of assessment projects in primary, secondary and post-compulsory education. He has been engaged in research into assessment and examinations for over ten years and, before going to Southampton, worked in the research unit of the Associated Examining Board.

Desmond Nuttall is Director of the Research and Statistics Branch of the Inner London Education Authority. He was formerly Professor in the School of Education at the Open University, where he headed a team producing the materials for the GCSE INSET exercise. He has also been the Secretary to a CSE board.

Harry Torrance is Research Fellow in the Assessment and Examinations Unit at the University of Southampton. He has conducted a number of investigations of teacher involvement in examining, and is particularly interested in the interrelation of curriculum, assessment and pedagogy. He is currently involved in a pilot study of a record of achievement project.

Preface

This Bedford Way Paper is intended as an introduction to the history, development, issues and problems of the General Certificate of Secondary Education (GCSE). The authors, who all have close links with teachers by way of teacher training or examining, hope that it will illuminate and open up some of the issues for teachers, teacher educators and others in education. It is not intended as a definitive statement about the GCSE, for things are changing all the time. Rather is it an account of the state of play and understanding of the new examining system in the second half of 1986. The next year or so will be particularly crucial in the implementation of the GCSE which is potentially one of the most significant educational innovations in the last fifty years, and will affect both state and private sectors alike.

There is much that is not well understood about the new system and not a little that is actually misunderstood. This is perhaps to be expected with something that is new, even experimental; which could be viewed as a Great Leap Forward or a Great Leap in the Dark, depending on one's point of view. And this makes an airing of the issues all the more important.

The titles of the papers explain quite clearly their content, so there is little need for editorial introduction, particularly in such a slim volume. Suffice it to say that the major issues tackled: differentiation, coursework, teacher assessment, grade criteria and the role and philosophy of the GCSE within the wider context of assessment at secondary level, are ones which the authors consider to be central to the future development of the GCSE.

C.G.
October 1986

GCSE: Some Background
Caroline Gipps

The development of a common examination
A detailed account of the history of the development of a common examination at 16-plus can be found in Nuttall (1984). I shall just attempt to summarize a major theme here: the desire of teachers and other educationists for a common examination at 16-plus, and then go on to consider the subversion of this concept through the introduction of differentiation. As Nuttall points out, there has been pressure for twenty years to merge O-level General Certificate of Education (GCE) with the Certificate of Secondary Education (CSE), indeed the first of these calls came only one year after the first CSE had been taken in 1965.

The CSE itself had been developed to cater for children who were not considered suitable for GCE O level, basically those in secondary-modern schools. Early suggestions that the pass level of the O level be lowered in order to accommodate the group of pupils in secondary-modern schools had, perhaps not surprisingly, fallen on deaf ears. Thus eventually the CSE examination was developed. Although the top CSE grade was linked to an O level pass in order to accredit the former, employers and parents never accorded the CSE the status which had been hoped for it. This in itself was disappointing, but, more importantly, the introduction of comprehensive education demanded a common examining system. The use of two examinations within the same school was bound to create problems of divisiveness together with organizational, curricular and administrative complications.

The irony is that 1965 saw both the first CSE examination and the DES Circular 10/65 which heralded the move towards comprehensive schooling. This, of course, was the result of the tremendous delay in getting the new examination under way: the proponents of an alternative public examination who started their battle in the mid-1950s could not have foreseen that comprehensive education would almost pip them to the post, and result in an inappropriate GCE/CSE split. This delay is, of course, mirrored by the delays in the advent of the common 16-plus examination, the GCSE.

It was in 1970 that the Governing Council of the Schools Council voted for a single examination system at 16-plus and, as a result, a huge development and feasibility programme was set up. The outcome was a report in 1975 (Schools Council, 1975) which said that a common system was feasible and proposed an examining system for the comprehensive school incorporating many of the elements of CSE, for example, teacher-developed examinations and an emphasis on assessment of course work.

As Nuttall points out, 1976 could hardly have been a worse time for putting to the Department of Education and Science (DES) a 'teacher-controlled and fairly liberal examining system'. This was the year in which James Callaghan gave his now famous Ruskin College speech which articulated public concern with 'standards' and heralded the start of a determined attempt to bring the government and the public into the business of education. What was wanted was less teacher control rather than more.

The rise of differentiation

Teachers' calls for a common examination in the 1960s and early 1970s were for just that — an examining system within which all the students who were entered took the same examination, having followed the same syllabus. However, the examination boards, test developers and educational measurement experts had always been conscious of the technical difficulties in examining over such a wide range of ability (Schools Council, 1971).

The 1975 Schools Council document described in passing the work of the small number of working parties that had attempted to devise an examining system rather than a single examination. By examining system they meant one in which there was either a choice of questions/papers of different levels of difficulty but with a limit on the grades that might be obtained via certain routes, or one in which a choice of content or method of assessment was possible but in which the full range of grades was available whatever the option chosen (Schools Council, 1975, p.19).

The first mention of 'differentiated' papers, however, came in the Waddell Report published in 1978 (Department of Education and Science, 1978a). When she was Education Secretary Shirley Williams had set up a committee, chaired by Sir James Waddell, to oversee an independent study of the joint 16-plus examination.

The report of the Waddell Committee echoed the 1975 Schools Council report by being in favour of a single system of examining, but it recommended that a range of papers be set designed to cater for the extremes of the ability range, which they termed differentiated papers. Having reviewed the trial examinations they felt that in some subjects the common approach was successful. In others, however, it was less so, particularly 'maths and modern languages' (interestingly science was not included in this group),[1]

> where the range of skills is wide and/or where certain concepts may be beyond the reach of many candidates. In such cases 'differentiated' papers are needed to enable all candidates to show what they can do and to allow the inclusion of items appropriate to some candidates only, without distorting the curriculum for others. (Department of Education and Science, 1978a, paragraph 30.)

These proposals were incorporated into a government White Paper in 1978 and one of the recommendations was 'to ensure that alternative papers are used wherever this is necessary to maintain standards' (Department of Education and Science, 1978b, p.11). Thus the notion of differentiated papers first appears as DES policy, something which seems not to have entered teachers' consciousness at the time. A National Union of Teachers' (NUT) document, also published in 1978 and responding to both the Schools Council 1975 discussion document about the 16-plus and the Waddell Report, makes no mention of differentiation.

The next important event was the change of government in 1979. The new Conservative administration was only tentatively in support of a common examination. The major concern was that a lowering of standards might result and, indeed, they wanted the examination to be tied to the standard of O level (Mortimore, Mortimore and Chitty, 1984/1986). Thus the notion of alternative papers of varying difficulty for different ability groups was to them an attractive one, and it now became a standard, if still relatively unnoticed, aspect of the proposals for a new system.

The next endorsement of differentiation in the 16-plus examination came in the Cockcroft Report on mathematics (Department of Education and Science, 1982). A general theme of this report was the importance of matching the level and pace of work to the level of attainment of pupils. This was considered to be equally important with the 16-plus examination. The report therefore commended the commitment in the 1978 White

---

1. It is pertinent to note that one of the DES secretaries to the Waddell Committee was a modern linguist.

Paper (Department of Education and Science, 1978b) to 'a variety of alternative examination papers and tests, at different levels of difficulty, in order to provide satisfactorily for candidates from the intended wide ability range'. The comments in the Report that:

> The syllabuses of examinations at 16-plus and the examination papers which are set should not impose inappropriate constraints on work in secondary schools. Pupils must not be required to prepare for examinations which are not suited to their attainment . . .

and

> there is far too little difference in the mathematics syllabuses which are followed by pupils of different levels of attainment.

are particularly important in the light of Sir Wilfred Cockcroft's move to be chairman of the Secondary Examinations Council (SEC) in 1983. A major role of the SEC has been the development of the new GCSE and given Cockcroft's commitment to differentiation it was unlikely that this path would be modified, supported as it was by an administration committed to education for an élite (e.g. the assisted places schemes, Crown schools, etc.) and whose major concern with the GCSE (as with the rest of the education system) was that 'standards' should not be lowered.

Given that the comments in the Cockcroft Report about not putting children in for an examination for which they are not prepared, or not capable of being prepared, make good sense, what is it about differentiation that seems to be a problem? Why are we raising differentiation as an issue?

The answer is that teachers wanted and originally thought they were going to get *a common examination* which would do away with the divisiveness of the old system. What they are actually getting is a common examining system (with the GCE boards responsible for the higher grades and the old CSE boards for the lower grades) with differentiated examination papers and/or questions in many subjects.

This has tremendous implications for teachers, not only in issues of supervising differentiated coursework (as the chapter by Macintosh below shows) but also in selecting pupils to follow different courses of work leading to different examinations, and in helping students to know whether to answer the hard or easy questions on an examination paper. Not to mention the technical problems of comparability of grading between a hard paper done badly and an easy paper done well. Indeed, a pamphlet published by the SEC in the Spring of 1985 (Secondary Examinations Council, 1985) recognizes that 'expertise in differentiated assessment will have to evolve gradually' — a statement to put fear into the hearts of those parents whose children will be examined in 1988.

Differentiation means that the system will still be divisive: that there will be separate routes to the examination; that some candidates will not be eligible for higher grades (if they take the less difficult route); that teachers will still have to decide which students are suited for which route/course/range of grades; that in some cases these decisions will still have to be made as early as fourteen. As the Cockcroft Report said:

> We have been given to understand that there are some teachers who are expecting that the introduction of a single system of examination at 16-plus will remove the necessity of advising pupils and parents as to the papers within the examination which pupils should attempt. However. . . those who teach mathematics must accept responsibility for giving such advice. (Department of Education and Science, 1982, para. 527)

If we set this against one of the arguments for a common examination at 16-plus in the 1975 Schools Council Paper, we can see that the debate has come full circle:

> At present, schools have to make difficult decisions on the selection of pupils for GCE or CSE courses, perhaps as early as the end of the third year. . . . Early choices cannot allow for the development of pupils' abilities . . . many teachers would say that the task . . . is one which they find particularly difficult and unrewarding . . . this practice may, to some extent, pre-empt the results of the examinations themselves . . . (Schools Council, 1975, p.9)

Ultimately, of course, any notion of a common examining system is weakened by the fact that the new examination still caters for only the top 60 per cent of the population in each subject, though of course since some students will be in the top 60 per cent for one subject and the bottom 40 per cent in others, many more than 60 per cent may take at least one GCSE.

Central control and the role of the APU

What are we left with, then, if not a common examination? There are still the important curricular reforms which the government, and many teachers, have been keen to introduce: the emphasis on practical work and assessment, teacher assessment of coursework and, as Goldstein and Nuttall point out in their chapter, a national syllabus (one would hesitate to call it a curriculum) enforced via national criteria. With regard to the last of these, there could hardly be a clearer, or more succinct, illustration of the development of central intervention over the process of schooling. By designing the product, or outcome, of schooling, the DES intends to shape the process.

Back in 1975 when the Assessment of Performance Unit (APU) was set up, it was viewed as a potentially dangerous DES initiative to gain *some* control over the curriculum via a national assessment system (Gipps and Goldstein, 1983). The, then unimagined and unimaginable, changes which have since taken place with the demise of the Schools Council, the setting up and governance of the Secondary Examinations Council and the way in which the GCSE has developed, means that the DES has achieved far more central control over education than ever the APU, could have done. As a controlling device the APU is of little use as we, and the APU pointed out in 1983. Only a sample is tested, schools and pupils are not identified, and there is no easy way of commenting on changes in performance over time.

However, the APU has had an input to the GCSE, indeed it could be said to have shaped aspects of it, in a way which we certainly did not anticipate in 1983. It has done this in three ways: APU survey information has been used to help develop the national criteria and more especially the draft grade criteria; methods of practical and oral assessment developed by the APU in mathematics, science and languages will dominate the GCSE practical assessments, for the APU is the only body to have recent widespread development experience of this; consequently, in-service training on practical assessment pioneered by the APU/DES will be crucially important in preparing teachers for this aspect of the GCSE. However, the APU practical assessments are essentially designed to operate with individuals or small groups; whether schools will have the resources required to operate practical assessments along similar lines remains to be seen.

Had the APU's development teams not pushed the development of practical assessment (spearheaded by the science group) one wonders whether the GCSE could in fact have gone for practical assessment straight away in the way that it has. Indeed the APU's science model with its emphasis on process rather than content has been largely adopted for the GCSE in science. Considering that the APU science teams were always conscious of, and concerned about, the impact of their assessments on the curriculum and therefore operated closely with the Association for Science Education (ASE) to produce a wide curriculum model (Gipps and Goldstein, 1983) this is probably a good outcome.

A quick look through the GCSE Guides for Teachers (Secondary Examinations Council/Open University, 1986) in science and mathematics will indicate the extent to which the APU's input has shaped thinking (although in the case of mathematics it is often via the mediation of the Cockcroft Report). Both these SEC Steering Committees had an APU representative on them.

The input of the APU to the development of grade criteria cannot yet be fully assessed (though their representatives were members of the committees in all appropriate subjects), but it seems likely that their national data on performance at 11, 13 and 15 will be crucial to the understanding of how children's competencies develop in mathematics, science, language and French. Whether or not this experience can be utilized, along with that from other areas such as graded assessment developments, will, as Murphy argues in his chapter below, depend a good deal on how further investigations into the development of grade criteria proceed in the next few years.

Teacher assessment: a cautionary tale
Teacher assessment of coursework is, as Torrance says in his chapter below, an important part of the GCSE, as it has been in CSE examinations. Of course there is a difference here in that in CSE, assessment was linked to teacher development of syllabuses in Mode 3 (as well as to board-devised courses), while in the GCSE there will be less opportunity for teacher-developed courses.

Whilst welcoming the formative nature of coursework assessment (contrasted with the summative nature of examinations), we should also sound a note of caution. Teachers' judgements of children's performance are subject to the bias which comes from stereotypes. This bias will affect not only the marking of coursework, but also the selection of children for different courses and papers.

As Valerie Walkerdine and her colleagues have shown, teachers' stereotypes of girls as 'not *really* bright', and 'working to their full potential' and their views of boys (with similar scores on mathematics tests) as 'really bright' but 'underachieving' (coupled with what society thinks about men being better at mathematics and science!) contrived to place the girls in CSE groups and boys in GCE groups (Walden and Walkerdine, 1985).

While teachers still direct more classroom attention and talk to boys and make their judgements about 'real brightness' on the basis of articulacy (Cullen, in press), then there is still room for bias in their judgements. For all its drawbacks, the formal written examination marked by an outside examiner, does avoid the pitfalls of stereotyping. Furthermore, unless positive work is done with teachers, girls are in danger of being entered for the medium or easy papers rather than the harder ones for which they may be suitable. If a common, i.e. single, examination had been possible then this would not be an issue. However, it is not a common examination, but a common examining *system,* and we must be aware, and beware, of its problems.

Criterion-related assessment: the Scottish experience

A very similar change in the 16-plus examining system has already taken place in Scotland. In August 1984 new courses of work started in English, mathematics, science and social and vocational skills, leading up to the new Standard Grade examination in 1986. Similar courses and examinations for other subjects will be introduced in two further phases.

In Scotland, as in England and Wales, the aim has been to move towards a criterion-referenced examinations system, and to bring about, at the same time, a number of curricular and assessment reforms. This can be summed up as a greater emphasis on practical and oral work in courses, more active involvement of the student in learning and more teacher assessment.

The Scottish teachers' action which began at the start of the 1984 school year had a major impact on the development of the new Standard Grade system. There was a boycott of in-service training:

> This was a particular problem for assessment, where Standard Grade had introduced a radically different approach and offered to teachers a professional responsibility in assessment which they had long sought but for which, in the event, many did not receive adequate preparation.
> (Scottish Education Department, 1986, para. 3.3)

Although it was the assessment element which caused most concern to teachers, the whole system has, in fact, been very complicated. Within each area of the curriculum there are between three and five assessment elements, or domains (e.g. practical skills, communication), and grades are given for performance in each element, thus giving a profile of performance. There are seven grades (for which grade-related criteria were developed) differentiated broadly under three levels of certificate examination (credit, general and foundation levels). Thus, within one subject, a student could follow a course at one of three levels and a Standard Grade Certificate could be awarded at one of seven grades on four elements; teachers may have had to assess pupils within all of these and in any combination. In addition teachers have to submit estimated grades for each pupil in each element on a 19-point scale, whereas under the old Ordinary Grade teachers simply had to produce an order of merit on a whole-course basis, and marks for any internally assessed component. The problem of grades for the elements has been exacerbated by uncertainties about the distinctions among elements which have been criticized as artificial in some subjects (ibid., para 3.9).

As a result of the concern felt by many teachers over the new Standard Grade system, a committee was set up under the chairmanship of Dr. E. McClelland, H.M. Chief Inspector for Scotland, in October 1985 to 'consider the scope for simplification' of the assessment and certification aspects. The Committee was popularly known as the 'Simple Committee' and it did indeed recommend a number of simplifications.

Among these is a reduction in the number of elements assessed; that continuous assessment be for feedback to teachers rather than certification, i.e. is less formal; that the grade-related criteria be defined only for three of the six levels of performance (the seventh grade simply indicates completion of the course); that the grade-related criteria be used to help teachers plan courses rather than used in assessment of the many tasks and exercises undertaken by pupils; that estimated grades be submitted on a 7-point scale per element rather than 19.

To conclude, the message from the Scottish experience would seem to be this: a system which is complex, albeit in an attempt to provide more useful information about students, may well be too complex to operate in schools. A system which makes heavy demands on teachers' time for assessment will be seen as taking time away from teaching. The curriculum reform which accompanied the Scottish examination reform was widely regarded as being beneficial. What the system fell, or rather hiccupped, over was its complexity and the unacceptable load on teachers. There must surely be a lesson here for the development of the GCSE.

References

Cullen, L. (forthcoming) in V. Walkerdine (ed.), *Girls and Mathematics: new thoughts on an old problem*. Milton Keynes: Open University Press.

Department of Education and Science, (1978a), *School Examinations: report of the Steering Committee established to consider proposals for replacing the GCE O level and CSE examinations by a common system of examining* (Waddell Report), Part I. London: HMSO, Cmnd. 7281.

_____ (1978b), *Secondary School Examinations: a single system at 16-plus* (White Paper). London: HMSO, Cmnd. 7368.

_____ (1982), *Mathematics Counts: report of the Committee of Inquiry into the teaching of mathematics in schools under the chairmanship of Dr W.H. Cockcroft*. London: HMSO.

Gipps, C. and Goldstein, H. (1983), *Monitoring Children: an evaluation of the Assessment of Performance Unit*. London: Heinemann Educational Books.

Mortimore, J., Mortimore, P. and Chitty, C. (1984; revised 1986), *Secondary School Examinations*, Bedford Way Paper 18, University of London Institute of Education.

Nuttall, D.L. (1984), 'Doomsday or a new dawn? Prospects for a common system of examining at 16-plus', in P. Broadfoot (ed.), *Selection, Certification and Control*. Basingstoke: Falmer Press.

Schools Council (1971), *A Common System of Examining at 16-plus*, Schools Council Bulletin 23. London: Evans/Methuen.

_____ (1975), *Examinations at 16-plus: proposals for the future*, Joint Examination Sub-Committee of the Schools Council. London: Evans Bros.

Secondary Examinations Council, (1985), *Differentiated Assessment in GCSE*, Working Paper 1. London: SEC, May.

Secondary Examinations Council/Open University (1986), *GCSE: A Guide for Teachers: Mathematics; Science*. Milton Keynes: Open University Press.

Scottish Education Department (1986), *Assessment in Standard Grade Courses: proposals for simplication* (McClelland Report). Edinburgh: SED, April.

Walden, R. and Walkerdine, V. (1985), *Girls and Mathematics: from primary to secondary schooling*, Bedford Way Paper 24. London: University of London Institute of Education.

The Sacred Cows of Coursework
Henry G Macintosh

Caroline Gipps in her opening contribution underlines the point which is essential to any real understanding of the GCSE, namely that it is not simply the putting together of GCE O level and CSE. Far too many people, however, still fail to appreciate this. As a result many of the 1988 GCSE examinations will not exploit their potential, particularly in relation to the provision of information about positive achievement in respect of all students. This, whilst unfortunate, will not be disastrous (the toleration threshold for change and innovation in education is in any case relatively low), provided that a process of continuing evolutionary change takes place over the next few years. As with the parcel in the children's party game, getting to the heart of GCSE requires the removal of a substantial number of layers of wrapping paper.

If evolutionary change is to take place naturally and without friction it will be necessary also for the ground rules by which we currently run public examinations to change. The criteria upon which the GCSE is based will have to be reviewed and where appropriate revised to take account of changes both within and between subjects and for teachers to reappraise their role in relation to the assessment of their own students. This means that both attitudes and procedures will require modification. Currently a great deal of new GCSE wine is being poured into some old O level and CSE bottles, some stronger, some more dilapidated, some even suffering from irreparable fractures. In such a situation a number of things could happen: new bottles could be designed; the old bottles could break and the wine flow down the drain, or the new wine could be diluted to suit the old bottles. The next few years will largely determine what happens to the GCSE and this in turn will determine the future of public examinations in England and Wales.

The significance of coursework

If one had to choose a feature of GCSE which encapsulated the points made in the opening paragraphs it would be coursework. This would form a part of everyone's list of significant features. Its potential is enormous but is as yet inadequately exploited largely because of the views currently held about coursework by teachers, the public at large, and examining boards. Before looking at the issues a number of general points about coursework need to be made. First, what is it? Very simply it is work undertaken during a course. It is not a method of assessment and may make use of any appropriate or inappopriate means of assessment.

The significance of coursework for GCSE is fourfold. First, it forms part of the criteria upon which student performance is judged in virtually every subject. Second, it is compulsory for all those in full-time education taking the examination. Third, it is intended to deliver the principle of fitness for purpose stemming as it does directly from the nature of the criteria themselves. And fourth, it carries a minimum weighting of 20 per cent. There is, of course, nothing new about coursework. It has always formed a part of classroom assessment and has constituted an element, albeit small, of many public examinations. Its rather restricted use to date has not, however, encouraged balanced consideration. People tend either to be for it or against it as a way of life and hence see it as an end in itself and not as a means to an end. It has not helped either that coursework has been more widely used in CSE than in GCE O level and this has caused it to fall foul of the British obsession for preferring to do worse on those examinations which carry greater prestige rather than to do better on those that are more useful.

Development of coursework models

This state of affairs has created a herd of sacred coursework cows which enjoy considerable prestige despite their dubious pedigree. Amongst the most influential members of the herd are Soft Option, Time Consuming, Finished Product, the twins Long Service and Good Conduct, and Teacher Unreliability. The messages conveyed by these animals about the current standing of coursework and hence its future possibilities are significant. Basically they are saying that coursework is all right for the less able and for soft subjects like sociology, but is inappropriate, even damaging, for able students and for hard subjects like mathematics. They imply also that coursework is extremely time consuming both for teachers and students and raise the basic question of 'can we trust the teacher?'

The coursework models available to the examining groups when they started to develop their GCSE 'syllabuses' were in the main extremely limited. They basically consisted of set-piece exercises or tasks, whether practical, oral or written, to which the name 'project' was often attached. In recent years these set-piece exercises have been improved in a number of ways; by allocating more time to the students, allowing them access to resources of varying kinds, by increasing the number of exercises and by making use of more specific criteria against which to design and to assess them. Some GCE Boards, in particular the JMB in a number of its A levels, have also developed checklists against which to judge work. Although these were intended primarily for moderation purposes they opened up possibilities for more integrated and continuous programmes of assessment.

Considerable refinement has also taken place in relation to projects notably in history, geography and the social sciences. More emphasis is now placed upon processes including topic selection, planning and evaluation often in conjunction with oral assessment, and less on the finished product. There have also been some interesting developments in relation to fieldwork in geography and in practical work in technology. These were accompanied by parallel work on moderation which initially involved little more than the sending of work through the post or visits from individuals employed part-time by the boards. To these were added moderation by consensus (of which the procedures adopted by the West Yorkshire and Lindsay and Southern CSE Boards and the JMB in its O-level English Language Syllabus D provide good examples), and the increasing use of statistics. The assumption underlying most moderation procedures particularly those for GCE has, however, remained that the judgements of teachers are unreliable. They therefore somehow have to be brought into line with the much more reliable external examination (yet another myth).

In the past two or three years examining boards like the Business and Technician Education Council (BTEC) and the City and Guilds of London Institute (CGLI) have made increasing use of problem-solving assignments in their pre-vocational examinations backed up by profiles, and often making use of log books which encourage students to take greater responsibility for their own learning. These assignments have a number of significant features:

1. They can readily be made cross-curricular in scope.

2. They can make very specific demands upon students and can in consequence be extremely practical.

3. They lend themselves to — indeed encourage — group work.

4. They provide a good vehicle for involving students in both their own learning and their own assessment.

5. They encourage progression and lend themselves particularly well to the demonstration of positive achievement.

Relatively little use of this approach to coursework assessment through assignments has been made to date within the curriculum covered by the GCSE, although the Schools History Project, with its five to seven assignments spread over two years and tied to quite specific objectives with equally specific criteria, is a notable exception.

Initial GCSE proposals for coursework
The emphasis within O level and CSE coursework has lain overwhelmingly with the use of a limited number (often only one) of time-defined individual set piece exercises occupying at most a half of a two-year course (a point which Torrance takes up in his chapter). These often place a heavy emphasis upon description and knowledge accumulation at the expense of thinking. This has resulted, particularly in CSE, in considerable student overload and in the production of much sterile and irrelevant material (long connecting paragraphs and glossy colour photographs which do not relate to the text, being much in evidence). It has remained rare for able students to be assessed on coursework. Moreover in certain subjects, for example mathematics, the entire assessment has been terminal for virtually all students despite the obvious potential of coursework for the really able who enjoy and profit from inventing and solving problems for themselves in their own time and at their own pace. A great deal of unprofitable time has also been spent upon systems of moderation which contribute little to improved teaching and learning and restrict valid approaches to coursework in the interests of largely unrealized reliability.

It is hardly surprising given this background that the early proposals for GCSE coursework have followed a similar pattern. In the Southern Examining Group, for example, coursework in history which counts for 20 per cent (the minimum) requires two written assignments each not to exceed 1000 words, one of which has to meet the empathy objective and the other the use of historical sources. The choice of topic has to come from within the syllabus. In home economics (family, home and food) the coursework which counts for 50 per cent consists of two parts, a written preparation (13 per cent) and a practical two-hour test (37 per cent). Inevitably the detail provided here is selective and superficial and hence unfair to those developing the syllabuses. It is also true that the SEG's English and science syllabuses provide scope for a variety of approaches to practical and oral coursework. The main thrust of the criticism, that the possibilities and potential of coursework in GCSE remain largely unexploited, is nevertheless a valid one.

Logistical problems and integration of assessment
There are however signs that this situation will soon change in response, initially at least, to a range of practical problems. The first two to raise their heads are ones that have already been mentioned earlier in this contribution, namely student overload and moderation. The volume of coursework prepared by subject working parties working (inevitably) on their own has meant that those responsible within the groups and at the Secondary Examinations Council for syllabus approval have had to take on board the issue of the total workload facing a single student taking, say, six to eight GCSE subjects. Incidentally it is only when a school considers doing this in respect of all its potential GCSE entries that the total resource implications of GCSE become apparent. The Southern Examining Group's initial response to this problem was essentially short term and took the form of requiring specific reductions to be made. Gradually, however, the basis of a longer term and more coherent strategy began to emerge. This included such things as the possible use of coursework for more than one subject thus permitting integrated coursework programmes, say on a faculty basis. Also the timing of coursework, or, put another way, could the coursework requirements be spread over the whole course differently for different subjects (they clearly could, although this inevitably raised questions of weighting, balance and aggregation)? Finally, there was the question of what might constitute the *minimum* evidence needed to make 'fair' judgements about student performance.

A similar logistical problem faces the examining groups in relation to moderation. The expense and often the impracticability of moving vast amounts of material or large numbers of moderators about the countryside has made postal or visiting moderation increasingly unattractive to the groups as a long-term solution. Statistical moderation of the type currently used and referred to by Torrance (see below) has been effectively ruled out by the subject-specific criteria, since the coursework is not intended to assess the same things as the more formal elements of the examination and there is in consequence no valid basis for comparison. Thinking upon these issues, certainly as far as the Southern Examining Group was concerned, was refined and helped by three things. First the production of the Secondary Examinations Council's helpful discussion pamphlet on coursework (Secondary Examinations Council, 1985a). This drew attention in outline to the range of opportunities available through coursework. Second, the emergence of a small number of syllabuses containing innovative coursework proposals. These often involved integration between subjects and were produced by people with little or no previous experience of producing O-level or CSE syllabuses. One of the most interesting of these was the 'Environment' syllabus currently being piloted prior to general availability in 1989 (Hawkins, 1986). Its coursework has a weighting of 70 per cent and consists of three elements. First, descriptions and response to places, both objective and subjective, second, the integration and evaluation of a social environmental issue and third, an environmental change project involving both individual and group work. The overall assessment is to be accompanied by a student profile. The third stimulus to thought was provided by the problems encountered by those preparing GCSE 'syllabuses' in developing differentiated assessment particularly where they wished to provide common assessment.

Whilst studies based upon the Schools History Project show that it is possible to use common written questions to test skills and concepts positively across the whole GCSE ability range (Secondary Examinations Council, 1985b), it has become increasingly clear that well-designed coursework programmes provide a potentially much more effective vehicle for achieving differentiation through common tasks across a wide range of subjects. Tailoring different exercises designed to meet the same criteria for different students is not an easy matter but is one which must be tackled if effective whole course assessment programmes are to be developed. Here again we need to reappraise the ground rules under which public examinations currently operate. Take, for example, the issue of assistance to students. Currently it is discouraged. Indeed in a written examination it tends to be called cheating. In coursework, however, the degree of assistance provided may contribute a perfectly valid basis upon which to differentiate positively among students.

Taken together these issues, which will continue to exercise all who administer public examinations, underline the irrelevance of much of the case law upon which coursework assessment is currently based and hence the need to put the sacred cows out to permanent grass. What is needed, instead, is to place a major emphasis upon whole course planning which will integrate assessment, whether formal or informal, terminal or in-course, with teaching and learning, and upon teacher accreditation without which the implementation of such programmes cannot be effective. If this does not occur then the new wine will indeed become diluted to suit the old bottles and GCSE will be unable to meet the curriculum needs of all students over the next fifteen or so years.

Teacher accreditation
Basically, accreditation means trusting teachers by underwriting their judgements in this case through the issue of a GCSE certificate to their students. Accreditation may relate to any aspect of course assessment and to the whole course as well as to any of its parts. It would seem, however, to be sensible as far as GCSE is concerned to make a start with the work undertaken during the course for this cannot in reality be assessed adequately without the teacher. It would also seem to make sense as a first step to start with individual teachers and then move on to departments and institutions. Harry Torrance in his chapter has addressed the key issues relating to the extension and development of teacher assessment. Unless these are resolved, and in my view this will not occur until the three questions of pay, conditions of service and appraisal are satisfactorily settled as a whole and proper recognition accorded to teachers as professionals, teacher accreditation will remain largely a vision. Its successful implementation will also depend upon the recognition by teachers that assessment in its broadest sense is an integral part of the whole teaching-learning process. Only then will increased competence in assessment be seen as an essential element of growth and professional development and lead to adequate training programmes which link curriculum, pedagogy and assessment and which can be used flexibly in a variety of intitutions. My purpose in the remainder of this chapter is to outline very briefly what might be involved in such a system in relation to GCSE. Without it coursework will remain a largely barren educational exercise in which far too much work will continue to be undertaken to little purpose.

The educational, administrative and financial advantages resulting from accreditation could be enormous. For teachers it could provide the opportunity to plan programmes within a national framework which were designed to meet the needs of their own students and to take account of their own expertise, interests and the environment within which they worked. For schools and colleges it could reduce, and eventually eliminate, the interference that external moderation arrangements, however well designed, inevitably produce. For the local education authorities and the examining groups there would be the prospect of linking in-service training in assessment with the requirements of the public examining system, and thus providing the degree of collective expertise essential to the establishment of public confidence in school-based assessment. Unless this is done the long-term prospects for developing credible records of achievement for all students will be severely diminished, and it needs to be remembered that this represents government policy for the end of this decade. All parties, but notably the students, will benefit from assessment programmes which place less emphasis upon bulk and gear themselves more directly to individual needs whilst remaining part of a national provision.

Looking forward
So much for the virtues of accreditation. How do we bring it about within the context of GCSE? As already indicated in the short run it is essential for the examining groups to develop moderation systems based upon consensus, as a platform upon which to develop the motivation and confidence essential for successful accreditation. Central to the notion of accreditation is the existence of a common bond, framework or set of rules — these may vary in detail or in terms of their prescription — between those seeking accreditation and those granting it. In the case of GCSE these would be the current relevant GCSE criteria. Those teaching a GCSE course and seeking accreditation (this must be something which people wish to undertake rather than something imposed from outside) would need first of all to satisfy themselves that their students had been provided with ample opportunity to meet the criteria. They would then need to identify and specify the evidence upon which they intended to base their judgements about student performance. This detail would be presented to and discussed with the accrediting agency, in this case the relevant GCSE group, and the latter would have to satisfy itself of its appropriateness.

The mechanisms, including the training provision necessary to facilitate accreditation and in particular the means whereby mutual trust and confidence can be established among all parties, will not be determined or achieved overnight. GCSE coursework, however, provides a golden opportunity for setting up a number of pilot schemes to establish these mechanisms and the Southern Examining Group has already started this process with one in oral English based at Bulmershe College. It intends to follow this shortly with another concerned with practical work in science. In the short run moves in this direction are bound to improve the quality of the educational provision available within GCSE and save both time and money. In the long run, however, they could be the first significant steps on the road towards freeing secondary education from the shackles of external examining. This would be both satisfying and ironic.

References

Hawkins, G. (1986), 'Taking on the pilot', *The Times Educational Supplement*, 27 June.

Secondary Examinations Council (1985a), *Coursework Assessment in GCSE*, Working Paper No 2. London: SEC.

────── (1985b), *Differentiation by Outcome in History — A Feasibility Study and Report*. London: SEC, unpublished paper.

School-based Assessment in GCSE: aspirations, problems, and possibilities
Harry Torrance

The expansion of school-based assessment — the assessment by teachers of pupils' practical work, fieldwork and coursework — is now an accomplished fact in GCSE. The moves towards more central control of the curriculum through the production of general and national criteria which might have been thought to threaten the existence of teacher involvement in assessment (cf. Bowe and Whitty, 1984; Nuttall, 1984) seem to have been more than counter-balanced by the new examination's stress on assessing what pupils 'know, *understand* and *can do*' (Department of Education and Science, 1985, p.2, my italic). As the general criteria and subsequent Secondary Examinations Council publications make clear, testing understanding and the practical application of knowledge must inevitably draw teachers more and more into assessment procedures since they are in the best position to make judgements about understanding and application; to test, in examining parlance, 'aspects of attainment which may not easily or adequately be tested by (final) papers' (Secondary Examinations Council, 1985, p.2). This 'settlement' in favour of teacher involvement in assessment begs two major questions, however, one of which I will mention only briefly since it is part of a wider discussion of the implications of GCSE for curriculum change to which I have attended elsewhere (Torrance, 1986a). The second will be the main focus of this chapter, building as it does on Macintosh's initial discussion of coursework.

If teacher involvement in assessment is to be construed solely in terms of examining — teachers being in the best position to conduct assessments and to mark work on behalf of the designers of the examination, the examining groups — then many of the benefits of school-based assessment may not be realized. In the past it has been claimed that teacher involvement in examining — especially through the mechanism of Mode

3 — has helped to facilitate curriculum development and to allow schools to develop courses suited to local needs and resources. But, of course, teacher involvement in school-based *assessment per se* — marking work under instructions from examiners — is not the same as teacher involvement in school-based *examining* (the *design* and assessment of courses within the school). It may be that teachers are placed in the position of unwilling conscripts, marking coursework against objectives and criteria defined and determined by others, further constrained by the widespread use of the assessment of coursework rather than liberated by it. Having noted this possibility, however, I wish to proceed on the assumption that the advent of coursework assessment is indeed intended to promote flexibility. Whether it does so in practice is another matter, of course, and this forms the basis of the second major issue which the expansion of school-based assessment raises: the extent to which teachers understand the rhetoric of the general criteria with regard to coursework assessment and the extent to which the rhetoric has any chance of being realized in practice.

The claims of the government and the SEC
The general criteria justify the inclusion of teacher-assessed elements in GCSE (and indeed all other assessment procedures) by referring to the principle of 'fitness for purpose'. Thus:

> all examination components and assessment procedures should reflect and be appropriate to the nature of the subject, its educational aims and its assessment objectives (Department of Education and Science, 1985, p.3).

Teacher involvement in assessment is thus treated as an issue of validity: the validity of the examination. This position is elaborated upon further in a section of the general criteria dealing specifically with school-based assessment:

> Internally-assessed components may serve one or more of the following purposes . . .
> (a) to assess objectives which cannot be assessed externally;
> (b) to assess objectives different from those for a written component;
> (c) to provide a complementary assessment of the same objectives as a written component;
> (d) to assess objectives for which there is only ephemeral evidence
> (ibid., pp.5-6).

Thus teacher involvement in assessment is grounded in the perspective of the designers of the examination. Irrespective of whether or not teachers want to become involved in assessing their pupils they are now being obliged to do so because the validity of the examination depends upon it (particularly the testing of objectives which cannot easily be tested by final papers — what pupils 'understand and can do').

A good deal more meat has been put on the bones of this justification by two subsequent pamphlets produced by the Secondary Examinations Council. The first of these continues to treat teacher involvement from the point of view of the examiner, but does so by drawing particular attention to the range of 'attainments' which might now be attended to by the new examining system (Secondary Examinations Council, 1985). The curricular aspirations of expanding school-based assessment are apparent by implication. Thus, for example:

> Some aspects of attainment which may not be easily or adequately tested by (final) papers are . . .
>
> (a) . . . making and recording accurate observations . . .
> (b) Research skills . . .
> (c) Interactive skills . . . ( ) . . .
> (e) Motor skills, including manipulation of apparatus . . . ( ) . . .
> (k) Attainment in tasks which, by their nature, require time for exploration: investigational, planning and design activities . . . ( ) . . .
> (m) Skills of adaptation and improvisation in the widest sense . . .
>
> (ibid., pp.2-4).

The pamphlet goes on to discuss the interrelation of curriculum and assessment more explicitly, acknowledging the examination's potentially dominant role:

> Coursework offers scope for developing an understanding of the part many school subjects play in the everyday world . . . and their relevance to pupils' own lives. Attempts within written examinations to assess awareness of the wider implications of a subject run the risk of being unfair because they depend on knowledge 'outside the syllabus'. But if a pupil is free to seek out the facts of a wider context this kind of understanding can be fostered and assessed (ibid., p.6).

The interrelation of curriculum, assessment and pedagogy is given even more prominence in the second and more recent of the SEC pamphlets (Secondary Examinations Council, 1986). Brief attention is paid to the general criteria, but the major justifications for school-based assessment in this pamphlet are construed in terms of curricular flexibility, responsiveness and relevance. Likewise it is suggested that 'teachers require guidance to ensure appropriate assignments and mark schemes are set which . . . will assess coursework positively' (p.3) and that 'teachers will not only be able to match students to assignments but also to select optimum performances which best illustrate positive achievement' (p.2). Here the argument has moved beyond that of validity *per se,* and the capacity of teachers to assess reliably that which it is deemed appropriate for them to assess, to encompass a wider debate about what should be taught in secondary school and *how*. The pamphlet goes on to discuss 'Formative and Summative Assessment' and 'Process and Product Assessment' (pp.4-5) highlighting the possibilities of 'learning through doing' (rather than just assessing the application of knowledge through 'doing') and also highlighting the concomitant positive impact which feedback to pupils on their strengths and weaknesses can have on learning. Even here, though, the traditional examiner's concern with issues of fairness which the assessment of coursework can raise, is apparent:

> Informal observation throughout a course allows a comprehensive assessment and an estimation of the extent to which students have *sought and received assistance* . . . (ibid., p.5, my italic).

The issue, then, is whether a real integration of curriculum and assessment can be achieved within schools or whether, because of the identity of GCSE as an 'examination' designed and organized by 'others' (the SEC and the regional examining groups), an uneasy dual role must emerge for teachers. This in turn brings us on to the role strain which teachers may experience as both encouragers and examiners of attainment; whether or not teachers have the knowledge and skills upon which school-based assessment will depend; and the logistical demands which the recording and reporting of assessments will make on teacher time and school resources.

Purposes and practices from the teacher's perspective

A good deal will depend on how the still emergent nature of GCSE comes to be perceived in schools: whether the notion of GCSE as an 'examination' becomes the overriding one. Clearly this is not just a matter of adequate in-service training and resource provision (important as these are); it will also depend on teacher's previous experience of school-based assessment and on the actual procedures which are followed by the different examining groups in the different subjects.

Previous experience is likely to have left many teachers with the feeling that 'coursework', because it has primarily been practised by the CSE boards, is more appropriate to some pupils — the 'less able' — than others. They are likely to regard the recommending of grades for coursework as a significantly different task to the routine assessment of coursework. That routine task could well have been at best a sensitive attempt to provide feedback and encourage revision and improvement of work, at worst a carrot-and-stick approach to classroom control through the accumulation and aggregation of marks (cf. Torrance 1985, 1986b). Such teaching strategies have been developed in the context of the broadly norm-referenced approach to grading which both CSE and GCE adopted. Classroom assessments have been made primarily in response to pupils' relative performance — compared with previous work produced by themselves and that of other pupils — rather than absolute performance. Teachers have responded to different pupils in different ways — sometimes using 'good marks' to encourage and motivate, sometimes using 'poor' ones to shock (and hence motivate!). Implicitly, therefore, different scales of marks have been employed for different groups of pupils, often within the same class. Occasionally this might even be explicitly organized with two pupils perceived by their teacher to be producing very different quality work being awarded similar marks, but with one pupil ultimately entered for CSE and one for GCE. Their sevens and eights out of ten would then come to signify quite different levels of achievement in the context of the two different examinations. How such practices will fare under a system which is claimed to be moving towards criterion-referencing, where marks can only be awarded for objectives achieved for absolute rather than relative performances, remains to be seen.

Previous experience with moderation — that process by which examination boards try to ensure comparability of standards across schools — will also have an impact on current expectations of the new system. Moderation has to date been organized on an end-of-course basis. This in turn has encouraged assessment to be construed as something which departments have to organize in the spring and summer of the fifth year of secondary schooling, with individual teachers pursuing their own practices until then, rather than as an important feature of a course which might best be organized in advance. A corollary of this is the enormous demands which end-of-course grading and moderation makes upon a school's resources in the late spring/early summer. Uppermost in many teachers' minds when school-based assessment is mentioned is likely to be the collection of work for coursework files, the re-reading of that work

— this time wearing the hat of examiner rather than teacher — the conducting of oral and practical tests, the attendance at internal and external moderation meetings. Thus whether or not school-based assessment in GCSE can be effectively pursued by teachers will depend upon a delicate balance being struck between the realization that school-based assessment can be utilized for a variety of reasons and is (as Macintosh points out above) appropriate for *all* pupils — something which on the face of it will mean an increase in the workload — and the realization that it cannot possibly be based on the current end-of-course procedures. To operationalize these current procedures properly would prove to be a logistical impossibility. Thus attention must be shifted towards some form of continuous assessment whereby the routine assessment of coursework can indeed provide the basis for ultimate certification.

The precise approach which examining groups and their subject panels adopt towards the organization and weighting of school-based assessment will therefore be of vital importance. Regulations which lay stress on the use of specially set coursework tasks, and perhaps encourage assessment situations which may seem easily controlled — the one-off oral or practical test for example — are likely to produce 'periodic' assessment rather than the continuous, flexible approach to teaching and assessment which might be claimed as the major *educational* justification for involving teachers more fully in the assessment of their pupils. As such, regulations which lay emphasis on closely defining the assessment situation and the teacher's role within it, in order to attend to the reliability and comparability of marking, run the risk of compounding the logistical problems of school-based assessment — setting special tasks, marking special tasks, recording and keeping safe the marks — whilst also denying the very logic of school-based assessment as outlined in the SEC pamphlets: that of the realism, relevance and appropriateness of tasks.

The related issue of weighting is also crucial. The examining groups may feel that too much responsibility is being thrust upon teachers too soon and, rather than grasping the opportunity to produce mainstream Mode I with significant elements of school-based assessment, may restrict its weighting to around 20 per cent of total marks, with larger elements of school-based work being undertaken through 'alternative syllabuses'. All well and good: teachers may be reluctant to take on the responsibility of marking large amounts of work for all their examination candidates and indeed may not feel particularly competent to do so. One can understand caution being exercised by examining groups and teachers alike. But if, in the longer term, the consequences of such decisions come to be that, for most teachers, their marking of coursework makes little or no difference to final grading because of the low weighting given to it, then teachers (and pupils!) are not likely to put as much effort as they might into making sure that the new system operates effectively. In turn, teaching methods and the overall orientation of the curriculum are not likely to change a great deal. Thus whether or not assignment-setting is treated as the complex pedagogical problem which it undoubtedly is; whether or not fieldwork and practical work command the space on the timetable which some might feel they ought; and whether oral work moves more overtly towards the centre of pupils' experience of schooling, will depend in large measure on the organizational practices which examining groups initiate. These in turn will solidify into the routine procedural identity of GCSE as curricular and pedagogical challenge, or bureaucratic examining chore.

Of course, as indicated above, teachers will still interpret GCSE in the light of their previous experience and mediate its impact on pupils. In this respect whether they have experienced involvement in school-based assessment as part of a wider aspiration to become involved in curriculum change could be important, since such involvement is likely to have given them a taste for the challenge as well as the chores of school-based assessment. While most teachers with experience of school-based assessment may have interpreted coursework assessment in terms of giving the 'less able' a 'chance', and may even have engaged in the development of Mode 3 schemes for just this purpose, some at least will have taken a rather broader view of the possibilities for curricular and pedagogical change which school-based assessment has to offer. Just as important, if not more so, many teachers will have developed a broader understanding of school-based assessment as the adoption of various new curricular packages (e.g. Geography for the Young School Leaver and Schools Council 13-16 History) have brought with them the need for individuals to teach and assess in different ways and for the development of at first unforeseen organizational changes such as team teaching and greater departmental planning and cohesion (Torrance, 1984, 1985).

Within these more positive experiences and working practices some of the more ambitious features of the SEC's aspirations may already have been realized. Pupils may already be working in mixed ability groups on well structured individual tasks, with assignments designed to call forth particular learning experiences rather than, or at least as well as, test understanding and application of previously acquired knowledge. But such good practice will have been developed within much more flexible teaching and examining situations than now seems to be being envisaged by the general and national criteria, and in an atmosphere considerably less fraught with the pressures of accountability than at present. Trying something new often means that mistakes will be made, coming fully to understand something new often depends on mistakes being made; to what extent teachers feel risks can be taken and mistakes tolerated under the new regime returns us to the question of the identity of GCSE which the examining groups present to schools. However much the proponents of GCSE may be interested in curriculum change, however much the SEC may wish to see the quality of teaching improve through the utilization of the flexibility which school-based assessment can provide, if the examining groups continue to treat teacher involvement in assessment solely in terms of the technical issues of marker reliability and moderation, then flexibility will be the least visible feature of the new system. And on this point, despite an initial focus on the issue of validity, the general criteria seem to leave the groups with little room for manoeuvre.

Moderating grades or improving teaching?
The general criteria construe moderation as a 'process of aligning standards between different examinations, different components and different centres or teachers responsible for the assessment of their own candidates' (Department of Education and Science, 1985, p.6). They further define the role of the examining groups in terms of the hierarchical generation, distribution, monitoring and approval of syllabuses, mark schemes and recording and reporting procedures. For example:

> The Examining Group *must* . . . scrutinize any question paper *or other assessment component* prepared by a centre or group of centres . . . scrutinize *and approve* schemes of marking; ensure that suitable guidance, in the way of assessment criteria, written instructions, group discussions, trial markings and training . . . is *given* to teachers . . . All systems of moderation of internal assessments must make clear the Examining Groups' *right* to *take such action as it thinks necessary* to bring internal assessments into line with general standards . . . (Department of Education and Science, 1985, p.7 my italic).

Exactly which level of the hierarchy is referred to here, what 'it' is, is a moot point, likewise how 'general standards' are to be identified and established. Overall, however, these sorts of injunctions are likely to mean that the logistical problems experienced in schools will have their parallels at group level, indeed we have already seen some of the consequences manifested in the late delivery of syllabuses to schools. To be fair, of course, we must reiterate the claim that the expansion of school-based assessment has been underpinned by a desire to render the curriculum more flexible and make examinations more valid. Indeed, the general criteria also stipulate that 'any scheme of assessment and moderation must . . . not be allowed to dominate the educational aims or inhibit good teaching and learning practice' (Department of Education and Science, 1986, p.6). But given the massive bureaucratization which is implicit in the DES attempt to give teachers greater responsibility and simultaneously to control the exercise of that responsibility, such a requirement is likely to prove at best a pious hope.

Further restriction is placed on the interpretation of these already very prescriptive arrangements by the acknowledgement of only two forms of moderation by the general criteria — that of statistical manipulation and inspection. With regard to statistical manipulation, attention is drawn to the necessity for some relationship to exist between internally and externally assessed components (so that the process of generating a correlation between the two involves comparing like with like and thus that variation can reasonably be ascribed to marker error). This sits uneasily, however, with our earlier observations of the general criteria promoting the expansion of school-based assessment in order to test those objectives and features of a course which canot be tested by final paper, and indeed to test more validly those which can. The alternative of inspection is also termed 're-aassessment' (Department of Education and Science, 1985, p.8) with the clear indication that it is likely to involve only end-of-course monitoring, quite possibly conducted by postal sampling rather than by moderators visiting schools. Having moderators visit school could at least ensure that work was re-assessed *in situ,* allowing them to appreciate something of the context in which it was generated. The two possibilities of statistical manipulation and/or postal sampling could well mean that teacher-recommended grades are changed in ways and for reasons which teachers will know nothing about. Combined with our earlier worries about the weighting of teacher-assessed elements, such procedures and their consequences are likely to undermine further any commitment which teachers might initially bring to school-based assessment.

Thus a much more flexible approach to moderation than has hitherto been practised, or is currently envisaged, must be brought into operation if teacher assessment of coursework is going to involve more than a vast, bureaucratic, badly conducted (and underpaid?) exercise in assessing work on behalf of, and under instructions from, 'the board'. By fostering continuous contacts across schools and between schools and the regional examing group, moderation could yet provide the forum for teachers to develop an understanding of, and an expertise in, both assessment and overall curriculum evaluation; to improve, in other words, the process of teaching, learning and assessment at source, in the classroom, rather than simply monitoring products at the end of a course. However this requires, firstly, a loosening of the DES and examining groups' allegiance to centrally determined, prescriptive criteria; secondly, the explicit recognition of school-based assessment as a mechanism for promoting curriculum development at school level not just for operationalizing the curricular intentions of central government; and, thirdly, very close liaison between regional examining groups and local education authorites (LEAs) over in-service provision and the utilization of moderation procedures for in-service work.

In fact, taking at least some steps towards such a situation ought to be possible even under the general criteria as they stand. Some form of 'consortium' moderation arrangements — under which subject teachers from groups of schools in reasonable proximity to one another can come together to discuss the syllabus, the work their pupils have produced, and the grades they would wish to recommend for it — could well be construed as 'inspection' and instituted under that general heading. Indeed, in the appendices to the second SEC pamphlet the Northern Examining Association acknowledges the possibility of organizing consortia, the Welsh Joint Education Committee 'anticipate' that they might develop, while the Southern Examining Group 'will allocate centres to subject consortia' in order that moderation can proceed on this localized basis (Secondary Examinations Council, 1986, pp.15-18). However, exactly what arrangements transpire and what practices become established, particularly in Wales and the North of England, remains to be seen. Furthermore, the Midlands Examining Group omits any reference to consortia while the London and East Anglian Group 'favours' postal sampling 'for the sake of economy, but also . . . to allow cross referencing' (ibid., p.12).

So prospects for a more flexible and 'curriculum-friendly' form of moderation are uncertain, but the possibility of groups of teachers coming together on a local basis to moderate each other's work does exist. Such moderation procedures provide the opportunity for teachers to discuss the products of coursework and by extension discuss the ways in which such products come to be produced, the teaching strategies and curricular organizations that gave rise to them. Similarly, once established, consortium arrangements can be used throughout the year to discuss teaching methods and changes in the curriculum. Such arrangements are not new and, as we have seen, they are going to form the basis of at least one examining group's procedures. However, in the past, individual examination boards have been moved to desist from such arrangements because of the logistical problems involved. Likewise, while consortium moderation has worked well in some areas, it has proved less good in others, particularly if treated as a rushed once-a-year event. Expanding school-based assessment will certainly not alleviate such problems and thus if the most is to be made of consortium arrangements greater liaison between examining groups and LEAs will be necessary. Time must be available for consortia to learn from disagreement, as well as to seek consensus, and to meet regularly throughout the year — certainly once, perhaps twice, each term — to discuss more fully, without the pressing necessity of grade agreement, teaching methods and curriculum change. Clearly such developments would require some support from the local authority, in the form of supply cover and so forth. But liaison could develop much further than this, with examining groups and LEAs perhaps jointly appointing moderators/advisory teachers on two or three-year secondments, to lead consortium discussions and integrate them into overall secondary in-service provision. Such liaison has already occurred in the GCSE in-service training programme. The 'subject-experts' which the examination boards were supposed to have at their finger-tips were in fact practising teachers and/or advisers with experience in examination work. Likewise the 'cascade' model, however mechanistic in conceptualization, has had to be adapted to circumstance, and a basis has been laid for group discussions across schools as well as for departmental training within schools.

Whether or not such novel forms of in-service support come to be provided there is no doubt that GCSE will call forth a range of in-service needs beyond those of simply assessing work for certification purposes. In particular new management roles will be generated for heads of department and faculty, and for the senior staff in charge of curriculum and timetabling. Faculty and departmental planning is likely to feature more strongly than hitherto, both with regard to the nuts-and-bolts of the impact of GCSE on staff and pupils — making sure that not everyone wants their coursework in on the same day, for example — and with regard to broader issues of balance and coherence in the approach to coursework which a school adopts. Time for such planning must be created and if it is done as part-and-parcel of moderation this may well give added impetus to a school's deliberations as well as in a sense redistributing resources from 'examining' to 'teaching'. In the first instance, of course, GCSE and the school-based assessment which it involves will stagger and splutter into life; anything else would be little short of miraculous given the circumstances of its launch. Simply operating new syllabuses and new procedures will be demanding enough at school level. But if the many educational aspirations underpinning the expansion of school-based assessment are to be realized, considerably more attention must be paid to generating an understanding of its curricular and pedagogical implications, as well as the examining and moderating problems to which it may give rise.

For the most part we still await the so-called 'phase four' of GCSE in-service training — the syllabus-specific training — as well as the 'effective follow-through and support' which the DES itself acknowledged was crucial in its initial letter announcing the GCSE training (Department of Education and Science, 1984). An opportunity still exists therefore to establish curricular as well as technical issues as legitimate topics of concern and debate. In-service provision which focuses exclusively on summative examining and moderating procedures is unlikely to prove of great use to teachers who are faced with the challenge of *setting* as well as marking assignments. Effective in-service work will need to be a continuing activity, feeding off and feeding into the actual setting and marking of work in schools. Arrangements must be instituted which facilitate this and contribute to the improvement of assessment practices in the classroom. If attention is focused solely on the mammoth task of monitoring marks and grades, it is a task which can only grow ever greater.

References

Bowe, R. and Whitty, G. (1984), 'Teachers, boards and standards: the attack on school-based assessment in English public examinations at 16-plus' in P. Broadfoot (ed), *Selection, Certification and Control*. Basingstoke: Falmer Press.

Department of Education and Science (1984), 'In-service support for GCSE teachers', letter from Sir Keith Joseph to Secondary Examinations Council, 21 December 1984. DES Press Release 217/84.

―――― (1985), *GCSE General Criteria*. London: HMSO.

Nuttall, D. (1984), 'Domesday or new dawn? The prospects for a common system of examining at 16-plus' in P. Broadfoot (ed.) op.cit.

Secondary Examinations Council (1985), *Coursework Assessment in GCSE*. London: Secondary Examinations Council.

_____ (1986), *Policy and Practice in School-based Assessment*. London: Secondary Examinations Council.

Torrance, H. (1984), 'School-based examining: a mechanism for school-based professional development and accountability', *British Educational Research Journal*, Vol.10, No.1, pp.71-81.

_____ (1985), *Case-studies in School-based Examining*. Southampton University, Department of Education.

_____ (1986a), 'GCSE and school-based curriculum development' in T. Horton (ed.), *GCSE: examining the new system*. London: Harpers Row.

_____ (1986b), 'Expanding school-based assessment: issues, problems and future possibilities', *Research Papers in Education*, Vol.1, No.1, pp.48-59.

The Emperor Has No Clothes: grade criteria and the GCSE
Roger Murphy

GCSE: a changing agenda?
As the first chapter showed, the move towards amalgamating GCE O-level and CSE examinations has a considerable history, dating back now nearly twenty years. One of the characteristics of this history is the changing nature of the issues that have been under debate. In the early 1970s many examination boards were running feasibility studies and trial examinations for a 'common system of examining at 16-plus'. These feasibility studies were evaluated by the Schools Council who, in its report in 1975, recommended the establishment of a common system as quickly as possible. This firm recommendation was greeted by a considerable period of foot-dragging and delay by the Department of Education and Science and a succession of Education Ministers. A few years more passed by while the Waddell Committee was set up and prepared its report. This report and the White Paper that arose from it in October 1978 heralded a new phase of the debate as the notion of national criteria 'emerged from almost nowhere' (Nuttall, 1984). The criteria were intended to ensure a degree of commonality among the syllabuses produced by different examination boards and 'to enable the grades awarded to be accepted with confidence by those concerned' (Department of Education and Science, 1978b). National criteria have in the ensuing years dominated much of the discussion and have become a 'key factor in determining the future of the 16-plus proposals' (Nuttall, 1984).

Thus, a debate about whether it was desirable to merge O level with CSE turned into a debate about the nature of national criteria that would be agreed upon as the basis for syllabuses for a new single examination system. One part of this new debate about criteria, which is itself beginning to develop quite a history, is an interest in going beyond defining criteria for syllabus contents to defining criteria for the performance of candidates that will be acceptable at the various grade levels for the new examination. This movement towards what has popularly become known as 'making the GCSE examination grades criterion-referenced' has in turn emerged as the latest and perhaps potentially the most radical of all of the debates that preceded it.

There has always been much confusion over how the existing CSE O-level and A-level public examination grades are reached. Each year, around the time the results come out, there tends to be a rush of heated correspondence about this topic in the newspapers. The grading practices are not quite as naive as is assumed by some of those who write in complaining that it isn't fair to fix in advance the proportions who will be awarded each grade. However, it is still a fair comment that the standards for the existing grades are at least based on normative judgements. For example, Grade 4 CSE has always been defined in terms of the achievements of an average 16 year old, Grades A-C of O level are usually awarded to about 60 per cent of the O-level entry, and Grade A at A level is reserved for about 10 per cent of the A-level entry. None of the boards follow these percentages slavishly, but from the annual statistics it is clear that they have a guiding influence on the overall grading pattern. Also, if one traces back to the first year of each of these examnations, it is clear that the original guidelines for grading them were expressed in this way.

The search for criterion-referenced grading implies an attempt to do away with all such norms and base the process of grade awarding on clearly defined standards expressed in terms of different types of achievement in relation to the subjects studied. Such practice has been commonplace in relation to the driving test, swimming awards and the graded music examinations in Britain for years. In each of these cases the underlying philosophy is that each individual is being tested against some fixed standards of achievement and graded accordingly. If 2,000 people all take the driving test in one city in one week, they can all be judged to have passed if they meet the necessary criteria. This test doesn't have a grading process based on the ethos that a certain percentage of applicants can be allowed to succeed and a certain percentage must fail.

The distinction between norm and criterion-referencing is probably fairly clear to all. What is much more difficult is translating criterion-referenced practices from relatively straightforward performance contexts (as in driving, music and swimming) into the much more complicated area of GCSE examinations with all their varied syllabuses and wide-ranging expectations in terms of pupil attainments.

The uncertain quest for grade criteria

Quite why the idea of making grades for the new examination criterion-referenced should have emerged in the early 1980s is open to speculation. It is certainly true that the criterion-referenced testing movement had gained considerable support in the USA and elsewhere in the 1960s and 1970s, but nowhere in the world had anyone attempted to apply the principles to large-scale national selection examinations like the GCSE.

Orr and Nuttall's (1983) excellent analysis of the early stages of the development of this debate in the United Kingdom also highlights the influence of the concern over comparability of examination grades that was prevalent in the 1970s. Both of these authors had been party to discussions with the Schools Council about ways of combating the perceived problem of a lack of comparability among the grades awarded by different examination boards. Undoubtedly the report from the Schools Council Forum on Comparability in the autumn of 1979, which strongly advocated the creation of 'national agreed definitions in terms of standards of work', must be seen as a very strong influence. Whatever the underlying reasons were, the official arrival of grade criteria into the 16-plus examination debate occurred in a written Parliamentary answer on 19 February, 1980. This ministerial enthusiasm for 'a single consistent system of clearly defined grades' arrived at through a process whereby 'all boards apply the same performance standards to the award of grades' was reflected in the letter that went out from the DES (28 February, 1980) to the boards inviting them to start work on preparing national criteria for twenty subjects.

The guidelines given to the boards at this stage were in many respects open-ended and flexible. The suggestion in relation to defining grades was that:

> Consideration should also be given to the possibility of incorporating (in the national criteria) some elements of criterion-referencing of grades, or some grades in the 7-point scale. This might help certificates to be more informative for users about the things candidates have shown they can do and go some way to free the award of grades from statistical norms of quality or performance change over time (Department of Education and Science, 1980).

Orr and Nuttall (1983) have documented the progress, or lack of progress, that was made on this issue during the next few years. The Joint Council for National Criteria, which was set up by the GCE and CSE boards, redefined the task that they had been given by the DES in terms of developing 'grade descriptions' for two out of the seven grades (Grades 3 and 6) that were envisaged for the new examination. Furthermore, the Joint Council distinguished quite explicitly in their own *Glossary of Terms for a Single System of Examining at 16-plus* in June 1981 between 'grade descriptions' and 'criterion-related grading', stating that one should not be confused with the other. Under *criterion-related grading* candidates would be 'required to demonstrate predetermined levels of competence in specified aspects of the subject in order to be awarded a particular grade' whereas *grade descriptions* merely attempt 'to indicate the levels of attainment likely to be shown by candidates awarded particular grades in a subject'. There is clearly a world of difference between these two approaches — a difference that the boards have recognized right from the start and one that the DES in time came to recognize as well. In a November 1982 policy statement on 16-plus examinations the DES publicly accepted the limited aim of producing grade descriptions for Grades 3 and 6 as a short-term objective only, but restated the hope that:

> Grade descriptions, as outlined above, may prove to be a step towards a longer term goal. The Secretaries of State have asked the boards to set themselves the objective of making the award of all grades conditional on evidence of attainment in specific aspects of a subject' (Department of Education and Science, 1982).

Thus, for the time being, the challenge of criterion-related grading had been dodged and it could happily be set aside as a 'long-term goal'. Perhaps in some people's minds this implied the 21st century at the earliest. At that time there were plenty of other substantial obstacles that needed to be overcome in a run up to the introduction of the new examination without taking on board anything as radical as criterion-referencing of grades.

Nothing more was heard of grade criteria for a couple of years until, in a bold last-ditch attempt, Sir Keith Joseph once again tried to inject them into the final throes of the GCSE development plans. The GCSE examination by then was being marketed as one of the major outcomes of his period of office as the Secretary of State for Education, and he undoubtedly wanted it to appear with all the trappings of the latest relevant technical developments. In April 1984 he announced in a speech in Bournemouth to the Assistant Masters and Mistresses Association that there was a need:

to supplement the Joint Council's national subject criteria, which are now nearing completion, with grade-related criteria if we are to achieve our objectives of enhancing standards, motivation and esteem. We need to define more precisely, for each subject, the skills, competences, understanding and areas of knowledge which a candidate must have covered, and the minimum level of attainment he must demonstrate in each of them, if he is to be awarded a particular grade. Pupils need to know the criteria by which they will be assessed. So also do teachers, further and higher education, employers and the public at large' (Joseph, 1984b).

This statement was followed up with other confident claims about what could still be achieved. Indeed, the development of grade-related criteria was mentioned specifically in the context of the announcement about GCSE in the House of Commons on 20 June 1984 as one of the four measures that would be part of a reform of the then current system of examining. Thus, the earlier warnings of the Schools Council (1979) and authors such as Orr and Nuttall (1983) about what a radical step this would be, together with the attempts of the boards to sidestep the issue, were apparently unheeded. A truncated timetable was announced allowing grade-related criteria to be drawn up in ten subjects so that they could be introduced into GCSE syllabuses for distribution to schools in time for the run up to the first set of examinations. This looked to some critics like a plan 'to replace the foundations of a new skyscraper with those designed by an unknown architect on the day before the official opening ceremony' (Murphy, 1984). It seemed inconceivable that the grade criteria could be added to GCSE syllabuses and schemes of assessment at that late stage without substantial alterations, and following the normal pace of development there was not going to be time for that.

For Sir Keith Joseph grade criteria, or 'grade-related criteria' or 'criteria-related grades', as they were alternatively titled as the months went by, were central to a move towards improving standards in schools. In his Sheffield speech of 6 January 1984 he said that if examination grades could be tied down so that they represented 'absolute standards of competence, skill and understanding which pupils of different abilities are expected to attain' (Joseph, 1984a), then it would be possible to set new targets at which teachers and pupils could aim. Later in the same speech he went on to suggest that it would be a 'realistic objective to try to bring 80-90 per cent of all pupils *at least* to the level now associated with the CSE grade 4'. Given that CSE grade 4 had always been norm-referenced, in the sense that it was supposed to represent an average level of attainment in a subject, this idea was rather puzzling. However, the general drift of the argument was clear: examination grades must be linked to absolute standards, which must be expressed explicitly in terms of clearly defined performance criteria, and then everyone must knuckle down to increasing the overall proportion of pupils who can satisfy these criteria. The first thing to sort out was the business of fixing the grades to criteria, and Sir Keith was determined to bring in this part of the innovation along with the new GCSE examination.

It is unlikely that many people involved in the developments that followed believed that such a radical step could be taken so quickly, since they recognized the immense difficulties involved in shifting public examination grades towards a system of criterion-referencing. Indeed, even before the first grade criteria working parties had got underway, late in 1984, their brief had been somewhat diluted by those within the Secondary Examinations Council whose task it was to advise them. In the space of a few words in the briefing paper that was prepared for these working parties, the Secretary of State's enthusiasm for absolute standards was watered down into a request for something that fell well short of criterion-referencing:

> The rigorous specification of full criterion-referencing for assessment in the GCSE would result in very tightly defined syllabuses and patterns of assessment which would not allow the flexibility of approach that characterizes education in this country. Nevertheless Council agreed with the DES that a move towards a greater degree of explicitness was desirable . . . (Secondary Examinations Council, 1984, p.2)

The late arrival of the reports of these working parties, the following summer, made the idea of introducing grade criteria into the first GCSE examinations less and less likely. When they were eventually published they were sent out to the examining groups for comment with a covering letter (dated 30 September, 1985) which emphasized the draft nature of the criteria and the fact that further work and/or pilot examinations should be considered as a possibility. Initial responses from the boards were requested by mid-February 1986 and these, predictably, reiterated the tremendous upheaval that would be involved in implementing the grade criteria at this stage. Like most of the education service, at this time, the boards were pretty well united in asking for more time and more money if they were to be expected to take this idea any further.

The Secondary Examinations Council appeared, at this stage, to have been positively encouraging the boards to argue that the implementation of grade criteria should be delayed. Their Annual Report for 1984-85 contained the following highly suggestive paragraph:

> It is clear to the Council that the employment of grade criteria will involve a further fundamental shift in teaching and assessment practices. The working parties have sought to identify the detailed skills and abilities which young people must show that they possess before achieving certain grades in the GCSE. Such explicit demands are rarely, if ever, made within current GCE and CSE examinations. It is not clear precisely when the first grade criteria will be employed within the GCSE. Much will depend on the response of users, especially the Examining Groups, to the feasibility and desirability of the draft proposals' (Secondary Examinations Council, 1985, p.14).

It was hardly surprising, with such a high level of collusion, that the threat of a rushed injection of grade criteria into the more or less complete GCSE syllabuses was at this stage countered.

Although at the time of writing no formal announcement has been made, it is now clear that there will be no grade criteria in operation for the first GCSE examinations in 1988.* Further work, however, continues and another ten working parties have been set up to develop grade criteria in additional subjects. Individual boards have also been approached by the SEC to carry out feasibility investigations, exploring how far grade criteria could be assessed through the existing GCSE syllabuses and schemes of assessment that they are planning to operate from 1988.

One notable feature of the latest stages of the grade criteria debate has been the lack of consultation. The draft grade criteria were never officially circulated to schools and teachers have not yet been invited to comment either on the general idea of introducing them or on the specific details contained within the proposals for individual subjects. This is both surprising and worrying, as it is clear that the introduction of grade criteria involves more than a set of technical assessment and grade awarding decisions to be made by examinations board officials. The curriculum implications of making explicit statements of the expected levels of attainment required of 16 year olds throughout this country are potentially enormous. The teaching profession and other interested parties should surely be given a chance to comment on such a move. It may be that this lack of consultation reflects a desire on the part of the SEC to make sure that grade criteria do not have much of an impact on GCSE as it has already been developed. It may be that the suggested move to criterion-referencing has been effectively neutered by the SEC and turned

---

* See note on p.53

into an almost irrelevant part of the trimming around the GCSE cake. The SEC appear to have been consistently steering the exercise away from criterion-referencing towards much more flexible criteria-related general guidelines. Once again this dates back to the guidelines developed for the first ten working parties, where Sir Keith's enthusiasm for 'absolute standards' was being subtly reinterpreted in terms of developing criteria 'to assist in grading rather than as absolute requirements' (Secondary Examinations Council, 1984). Thus in the eyes of the SEC, anyway, there is a marked distinction between grading on the basis of grade criteria and criterion-referenced grading.

Whether grade criteria that are developed along the SEC lines will be worth the paper that they are printed on, and make any significant impact at all, remains to be seen. It is certainly the case that they are unlikely to allow the users of examination grades to have an 'assurance that pupils obtaining a particular grade will know certain things and possess certain skills or have achieved a certain competence' (Joseph, 1984a).

When the idea of criterion-referencing examination grades was first introduced into the debate about national criteria for GCSE it was deflected by a move from the boards to develop 'grade descriptions'. Four years on we are now looking at slightly less watered down proposals which still involve a good deal of flexibility and compensation. At one stage in the debate about how grade criteria would actually operate Secondary Examinations Council staff were said to be talking about a system involving 'flexible soft-topped hurdles', which would allow candidates to fail to meet certain criteria but still gain the overall grade which was supposed to be based on the mastery of these criteria. If this is what is now understood by 'criterion-referenced grading' then in actuality we may not be moving very far from time-honoured, but somewhat arbitrary, grade awarding practices. As Christie and Forrest (1981) have outlined, public examination grading has always involved the use of some performance criteria, however vaguely and flexibly these may have been interpreted, as they have been used in conjunction with norm-referenced statistical information to determine the final cut-off scores for individual grades.

Grade criteria: the way forward?

Considerable doubt has to remain concerning the dual issues of whether or not a major shift can be made towards making the grading of public examinations criterion-referenced, and what impact this would have on both teaching and learning and assessment procedures. It has certainly become clear that such a move involves fundamental changes in the whole structure of the present examination system and the evidence that is beginning to emerge from Scotland (for example see the McClelland Report (Scottish Education Department, 1986) and the first chapter above), where developments in this direction have moved ahead somewhat faster, will increase rather than decrease the fears and the doubts in the minds of those involved in considering these changes south of the border.

It has been apparent for a long time that the introduction of grade criteria cannot be approached by bolting-on a further set of 'designer-produced' fancy accessories to existing examinations and syllabuses. At the present time candidates who attain the same grade in GCE and CSE examinations do so on the basis of an enormously different range of performances in these examinations (Kempa and L'Odiaga, 1984; Jones and Murphy, 1984).

The work that is currently going on to develop domains within individual subjects and sets of specific attainments within those domains is a step towards developing an alternative approach. There are, however, some fundamental problems that will have to be addressed if such a system is going to be introduced into GCSE at some later date, presumably in the 1990s. First and foremost curriculum-related questions need to be asked about the proposed domain structures of the subjects: for example, the extent to which the division of GCSE syllabuses into domains and lists of specific achievements is appropriate and desirable, and the type of impact that these will have on teaching and learning and examining. Secondly, there are some substantial technical assessment problems that need to be solved concerning approaches to assessing and grading within a system of criteria broken down into domains. Each individual criterion would have to be studied in terms of how it can be assessed and how precisely an expected level of attainment can be described by it. Then there is the problem of combining information from the assessment of a large number of individual criteria. How will domain grades be arrived at, and how should these be presented or combined? The Secondary Examinations Council has already stated a preference for the production of 'a profile of performance across the domains of a subject as well as the overall grade' (Secondary Examinations Council, 1985, pp.13-14). One is immediately tempted to consider the relationship between this profile and others that are going to be produced under the DES 'Records of Achievement' intiative. If, from 1990, all school leavers are to have a school-leaving profile or record of achievement, can this be based at least partly on statements related to the achievement of nationally recognized GCSE grade criteria?

If grade criteria are to be introduced into GCSE syllabuses they will undoubtedly have major implications for teachers as well as the examining boards. Quite apart from the curriculum influences that have already been mentioned, there is the question of the impact on the coursework assessment procedures that are an integral part of the new GCSE schemes of assessment. Clearly the basis for assessment within these will have to be linked to any grade criteria that are introduced and, if teachers are expected to take on board a fundamental shift in their assessment procedures, a further programme of in-service training will be needed.

The search for criterion-referenced grades for the GCSE is not necessarily a forlorn one. There is much relevant experience that could be used, for example that gained through graded assessment developments (see Murphy and Pennycuick, 1986). If the desire to alter fundamentally the basis for grading 16-plus examinations is a sincere one then the objective is attainable. It will require some very detailed research investigations to explore the full range of possibilities that will need to be considered in order to have any hope of arriving at a workable solution. Undoubtedly these will involve a wider range of assessment procedures than are currently being considered for the first GCSE examinations. It will also be necessary to develop the existing draft grade criteria in relation to the results of such research investigations.

Whether or not there will be an interest in conducting the kind of fundamental research that would be needed in order to move towards criterion-referenced public examinations remains to be seen. The initial proposals that have been put forward by the SEC for follow-up research in relation to the draft grade criteria are very limited, and are largely concerned with exploring whether existing GCE and CSE examination papers could be marked by examiners using the draft grade criteria instead of their usual marking schemes. Such research sets severe limitations on the amount of change that can be contemplated in relation to a move towards introducing grade criteria, and is doomed from the start. Any real move towards considering the introduction of grade criteria, in such a way that the GCSE will genuinely become criterion-referenced, will need to involve a much more fundamental reconsideration of the methods of assessment to be used, and the nature of the syllabuses to which they will relate. Finally, it would be necessary to follow up such changes by a further period of in-service training for teachers who would need to prepare their own GCSE activities from a quite different standpoint.

It may well be that something much less fundamental than this will occur. If it does it is likely to be in the form of a further token gesture that will reaffirm the 'long-term objective' of introducing criterion-referenced grading without actually moving very far in that direction. For the time being the grade criteria have taken on a resemblance to the Emperor's clothes: there aren't going to be any on the day of the parade, but any mention of that fact may cause a little embarrassment in certain circles.

Note

A letter from the Secretary of State for Education and Science to the Secondary Examinations Council and a DES Press Release (256/86), both dated 2 October 1986, have subsequently confirmed that the grade criteria will not be in operation by 1988. The Secretary of State, however, calls for 'rapid progress' in completing the development work so that at least some 'trial examinations' accommodating grade criteria can be held in 1989.

References

Christie, T. and Forrest, G.M. (1981), *Defining Public Examination Standards*. London: Macmillan.

Department of Education and Science (1978a), *School Examinations, report of the Steering Committee established to consider proposals for replacing the GCE and CSE examinations by a common system of examining* (Waddell Report). London: HMSO.

―――― (1978b), *Secondary School Examinations; a single system at 16-plus*. London: HMSO.

―――― (1982), *Examinations at 16-plus: a statement of policy* London: HMSO.

Joint Council for National Criteria (1981), *Glossary of Terms for a Single System of Examining at 16-plus*.

Jones, A. and Murphy, R.J.L. (1984), 'The development of grade-related criteria for GCSE examinations' in *Targets in Science*. London: Secondary Examinations Council.

Joseph, Sir Keith (1984a), Speech at North of England Education Conference. Sheffield, 6 January. DES Press Release 1/84.

_____ (1984b), Speech to Assistant Masters and Mistresses Association, Bournemouth, April. DES Press Release 65/84.

Kempa, R.F. and L'Odiaga, J. (1984), 'Criterion-referenced interpretation of examination grades', *Educational Research,* Vol.26, pp.56-64.

Murphy, R.J.L. (1984), 'Mission impossible', *The Times Educational Supplement.* 30 November.

Murphy, R.J.L. and Pennycuick, D.B. (1986), 'Graded assessments and the GCSE' in T. Horton (ed.), *GCSE: examining the new system.* London: Harper & Row.

Nuttall, D.L. (1984), 'Doomsday or a new dawn? The prospects for a common system of examining at 16-plus' in P.M. Broadfoot (ed.), *Selection, Certification and Control.* Basingstoke: Falmer Press.

Orr, L. and Nuttall, D.L. (1983), *Determining Standards in the Proposed Single System of Examining at 16-plus,* Comparability in Examinations Occasional Paper 2. London: Schools Council.

Schools Council (1979), *Standards in Public Examinations: problems and possibilities,* Comparability in Examinations Occasional Paper 1. London: Schools Council.

Scottish Education Department (1986), *Assessment in Standard Grade Courses: proposals for simplification* (McClelland Report). Edinburgh: SED.

Secondary Examinations Council (1984), *The Development of Grade-Related Criteria for the General Certificate of Secondary Education. A briefing paper for working parties* London: SEC.

_____ (1985), *Secondary Examinations Council Annual Report 1984-85.* London: SEC.

Can Graded Assessments, Records of Achievement, and Modular Assessment Co-exist with the GCSE?
Harvey Goldstein and Desmond L. Nuttall

Philosophical considerations
The other chapters in this volume describe and evaluate various aspects of the GCSE. Here we look at the relationship between the aims of the GCSE and those of other major assessment initiatives — graded assessments and records of achievement. Furthermore, since the focus of this volume is the GCSE, we do not consider the possible operation of graded assessments or records of achievement independent of GCSE or as the dominant modes of assessment, although this is not to deny that either (or both in partnership) might eventually predominate at least at some levels of education.

We shall describe each of four types of assessment (graded assessments, records of achievement, modular assessments and the GCSE) in terms of their educational justifications, followed by an analysis of the implicit and explicit educational philosophies embodied in these justifications. From there we shall draw out the similarities and conflicts between the types, and hence the issues likely to emerge in any simultaneous implementation of one or more of the types of assessments in the same educational environment alongside GCSE.

A major difficulty we have found in discussing philosphical or theoretical foundations is that there is very little serious attempt to relate any of the current initiatives to existing educational philosophies or to indicate the outline of a new one. Thus, the graded assessment movement draws much of its inspiration and rhetoric from graded tests in other areas, notably in artistic and sports fields, but with minimum critical analysis of the similarities and differences between those areas and general education in schools. Records of achievement are commended to us as providers of a wider portfolio of information, without addressing the question of the optimum amount of information that is required for different purposes. In similar vein, the new GCSE, as might be anticipated from an essentially bureaucratically driven exercise, deals with the notion of 'standards' by abandoning a critical definition in favour of metaphor.

Part of our task, therefore, has been to infer key features of the frameworks within which advocates of the different assessments implicitly seem to operate. Yet our aim is not to engage only in philosphical argument, but to use that to prepare a practical critique. If the result appears unduly critical, then we make no apology but rather invite those who do not share our conclusions to join us in a debate we feel is long overdue. We should also make it clear that we accept that the very fact of change often produces new perspectives and hence important innovations in curriculum and teaching. Undoubtedly this is true of new assessment approaches. Our concern here, however, is to examine the specific claims of these approaches rather than their effects, which are often beneficial if sometimes unplanned or unexpected.

Graded assessments
The early discussion of graded testing or assessment often involved reference to graded examinations in music or grade certificates awarded for swimming, etc. (see, for example, Harrison, 1982). The advantages of such assessments were said to be in the short-term 'positive' motivation provided by relatively clearly defined tasks to be 'mastered', or competencies to be demonstrated. The term 'positive' refers to the reinforcement provided by a high probability of 'passing' a grade, which in turn implies that students are not entered unless they are perceived to have a high probability of passing. Thus the 'positive' nature of the assessment resides in appropriate entry decisions rather than in the assessment itself, and so depends upon the actions of teachers and others. If this is so, then at the very least we need to have an understanding of how the mechanism works, if indeed it does, in other parts of the curriculum. Furthermore, what are the procedures whereby pass rates are maintained and how do these react upon teaching and learning? Such questions lead to broader ones about the relationships between tutor and student, about whether there is an inherent link between this relationship and the form of assessment, and about whether the assessment method can be 'lifted' from one context to another. Of particular interest is the question of how 'negative' achievement or 'failure' is dealt with. We shall return to these issues, and also what we call context-related assessment, below.

The second common aspect of graded assessments is the acceptance of the idea of 'mastery'. Because of its often close association, or even identification, with the notion of criterion-referencing we shall be discussing the two together below. We note, however, that both notions relate explicitly to a body of educational writing largely concerned with the formulation of detailed, and usually behavioural, educational goals and methods of assessing the achievements of those goals (e.g., Bloom, Hastings and Madaus, 1971). In practice, however, this literature tells us little about how to operationalize notions of mastery in relation to broad-based curricula as opposed to narrow definitions of skill; consequently, the development of graded assessments has been *de novo,* rather than part of any systematic extension or application of the existing theory of mastery learning and assessment.

The use of the results of graded assessments does not seem to have been fully thought through. Apart from their obviously redundant use in deciding whether to proceed to the next 'level' of assessment (given the policy governing entry decisions), the results of many graded assessments are to be equivalenced to a grade level of GCSE. This has been unashamedly justified in order to achieve acceptance and 'respectability' for graded tests, and there has been little examination of the consequences of such equivalencing. It is tacitly assumed that it can be done without prejudicing existing aims, but this is not guaranteed and we shall examine this further when we discuss the nature of assessment instruments when they are required to perform a selection function.

Finally, an issue which afflicts all assessment procedures (perhaps more in the United Kingdom than elsewhere in the world) is that of *comparability* — across time as the content of the assessment changes, across institutions such as schools which use different content and contexts to assess the same objectives, and across domains or subjects. The only known areas where comparability or equating can be said to work are very narrowly defined cases involving costly norm-referenced procedures, hardly applicable to the schemes being developed (see Holland and Rubin, 1982; Goldstein, 1986). Yet the descriptions of graded assessment schemes are predicated on a common understanding of what each level 'means'. What is unclear is the epistemological basis for such meaning — is the intention to 'objectify' it in terms of mathematically-defined relationships as in test equating, or to refer it to expert judgement, or perhaps simply to ignore the problem by pretending it does not exist? We shall have more to say about this later.

Records of achievement
A principal distinguishing feature of records of achievement (or profiles) is their incorporation of explicit and separate assessments of a much wider

range of achievements than other modes of assessment, especially in the affective domain. It is, however, worth remarking that there appears to be no reason why such achievements should not be incorporated into the other three forms of assessment. That this appears not to have been seriously considered reflects the provenance of graded assessments, modular assessments and the GCSE and their primary concern with the same set of issues. The main appeal of profiling is to the notion of education for the whole person, to a desire to give positive value and status to affective and other non-academic achievements. For many, the real value of this appeal is to the teacher and above all to the student himself or herself and lies in the *process* of education, and the control of teacher and student over the assessment. But few deny (albeit reluctantly in some cases) that status can be conveyed only by means of a permanent, observable record negotiated between student and teacher. It is this record which, along with the other kinds of assessment, would be 'used' . . . by whoever wants to use it. Clearly, to achieve value for non-cognitive activities, knowledge of them has to be of use to someone. Yet we find little explicit discussions of who that person (other than the student) is, but there seems to be a general presumption, as in the Oxford Certificate of Educational Achievement (OCEA), that it is a selector of sorts — an employer, perhaps, or a Youth Training Scheme (YTS) managing agent. So again we find an instrumental end-product, raising the issue we mentioned above of the way in which the use of an assessment interacts with its initial philosophy. A fundamental question is how far the ideal of honest and objective recording is compatible with the reality of knowing that such recording may have a role in determining life chances. This is hardly a novel question, but it still deserves a considered response.

Two other important issues arise with records of achievement which have counterparts in the other forms of assessment. The first is made explicit in many of the profiling systems (e.g. those of the City and Guilds of London Institute) that consist of graded descriptions of each of a wide range of achievements. A key feature of these is their out-of-context formulation, that is, their phrasing in terms that sound very much like general 'skills' or 'abilities' presumed to exist independently of any particular context. Here, a direct line of descent can be traced from a traditional and widely held belief in such concepts as 'intelligence', though this belief is one that has increasingly been questioned. Yet if such descriptions convey little real information, is it then possible to generate records of achievement in terms of context-specific descriptions?

The second issue is again that of 'positive' achievement. If negative comment is to be eschewed (as the Department of Education and Science (1984) advocates), 'negative' achievement presumably becomes that range of possible achievements which are not mentioned in the record. There would seem to be a clear invitation to read between the lines, and this leaves us wondering what the term 'positive' achievement really signifies.

Modular assessment
A number of different arguments are put forward for breaking up a course of study into relatively small units or modules, and assessing achievement at the end of each. One argument is for curricular flexibility (and sometimes organizational flexibility) so that students can have more choice, and a greater variety of potentially valuable courses can be created. But where the modules are being combined to create courses for the GCSE examination (as is the case in many TVEI schemes), the national criteria tend to create a straitjacket and much of the curricular flexibility is lost because only a very limited number of combinations of modules will be acceptable as a GCSE course in physics, say.

Some modular schemes (such as those operated by the Business and Technician Council and the Open University) consist of modules that are studied over a period as long as a year. Other schemes (e.g. Inner London Education Authority, 1984) advocate modules that can be completed in as little as six or eight weeks, so that students receive relatively rapid public feedback about performance. In this they resemble graded assessments, but the assumption is that the students will be assessed when their group completes the module, rather than when they are individually ready. Many will therefore fail (or show modest achievement); the consequence that many students will have more negative than positive reinforcement does not seem to have been faced.

Modular schemes often share many of the features of the other assessment initiatives, such as criterion-referencing and the specification of detailed objectives or assessment criteria that are independent of context. But modular schemes experience the problems of comparability in a much more acute form than other types of assessment when aggregated for the purpose of some global award like a degree or a GCSE grade. If curricular flexibility is to be encouraged, then students will present a great variety of different combinations of modules, but the assumption will usually have to be made that a grade 2, say, in one module is equivalent to a grade 2 in any other module. The more that choice is constrained (as it will be in GCSE, as argued above), the more the problem is alleviated, but the greater the loss in flexibility.

The GCSE

At the heart of the GCSE proposals is the aim of specifying curriculum content and pedagogy by a suitable specification of the examination system. (for the detailed argument see Nuttall, 1984). Of course, for any examination system to be able to succeed in this task, it must possess sufficient muscle to have its way. Historically, in Britain, there has been little doubt, even among its bitterest opponents, that the public examination system really matters to parents, students, teachers, further and higher education, and employers; that same cultural assumption has clearly been inherited by the GCSE. As we have already said, at least two of the other forms of assessment currently being developed look to the GCSE to legitimize their own status.

We should make it clear that we do not take a value position when we talk of examinations determining aspects of curriculum and pedagogy. We believe that there should be a debate on the extent to which this is desirable, and about other approaches to curriculum determination and control (described, for example, by Broadfoot, 1979). That debate is not being held now and may well be irrelevant once the GCSE is in place.

Other contributions to this volume analyse the significant features and innovations of the GCSE. Here, then, we summarize their effects upon schools, teachers and students. The aims, objectives and content of examination courses are determined (with varying precision in different subjects) by the national criteria (Department of Education and Science, 1985). Although there is provision in the criteria for their regular review and for their temporary suspension to allow for promising curricular developments to be tried, they will be difficult and time-consuming to modify. (At the time of writing, the criteria have been suspended only for one subject, SMP mathematics, a subject dear to the hearts of the top brass of the Secondary Examinations Council.) The advent of grade criteria would lead to a tightening of the specification of the curriculum. Curricular and classroom organization will be determined partly by the need to prepare students for a particular 'level' of the examination in many subjects (see Gipps's chapter above), somewhat in the present manner of choosing CSE or GCE, but possibly with a finer gradation; partly by the need for coursework and its assessment (see Macintosh's chapter); and partly by the grade criteria (see Murphy's chapter). Pedagogy stands to be influenced by the increased involvement of teachers in the process of assessment (see Torrance's chapter). Because of the requirement for comparability and the consequent need for some kind of moderation of teachers' and pupils' work, the traditional role relationship of teacher and learner seems destined to be nudged in the direction of formal assessor and candidate, with possibly profound implications for traditional roles and with penalties for departures from the new role. We shall return to all of these core issues when discussing practical implications.

Selection and assessment
In common with existing 16-plus examinations, the principal use of the GCSE is as a selection device, whether for employers or as a requirement for training courses or advanced educational studies. The primacy of this function has particular consequences. We have mentioned already the way in which the other forms of assessment, directly or indirectly, aspire to gain a share of the action and we have alluded to the way in which this changes their role. The role of the 16-plus examination itself reflects the deeper commitment of the secondary education system to selection and much of past and present debates can be said to be concerned with the tension between the selective and other functions of education (see Broadfoot, 1979). What seems to be emerging at the end of the 1980s, however, is a willingness on the part of those concerned with devising new modes of assessment to concede that the credibility of these new modes is dependent upon accommodating to the GCSE and to the demands of the user outside the school gates — in effect, to concede the primacy of selection, albeit with extreme reluctance and distaste in some cases. It is because of the many ways in which graded assessments, modular schemes and records of achievement are having to make compromises that we feel that their initial beneficial effects within schools and classrooms cannot yet be taken as established.

In many ways, graded assessment and profiling are attempts to formalize much of the teacher-initiated informal assessment of learning which takes place as an inherent part of teaching. Such informal assessment may take a variety of guises, but its aim is formative which distinguishes it from assessment for selection, which is invariably summative. Indeed, the policy of some schools and teachers is consciously to postpone as far as possible the time at which the latter mode of assessment begins to dominate. This leads us to ask what we believe is a key question underlying all current developments, namely how far the acceptance of the supremacy of the idea of 'assessment for selection' militates against any change in the nature of teaching and learning in schools. It is not our purpose to offer speculative answers to this question, but rather to place it onto an agenda for debate. It is, of course, the striving for fairness in selection that puts such emphasis upon comparability and reliability, and permits the down-grading of what should be pre-eminent, namely validity.

Criterion referencing
The notion of criterion-referenced assessment has acted as a principal legitimating device for the GCSE and to a lesser extent for graded assessment and records of achievement. The idea that the result of an assessment enables you to say 'what a student can do' rather than 'how a student is ranked in relation to her peers' is seen as an attractive one, and has inspired much research and debate over the past twenty years. Much of this debate has been concerned with the relationship between assessment and the curriculum, the clear specification of assessment objectives, the predictive generalizability of such assessments and the problem of defining a suitable criterion 'level' for deciding whether the 'can do' description can be awarded, and in what contexts.

It could be argued that the clear specification of assessment objectives is a desirable feature of all assessment procedures, as is an understanding of the predictive usefulness of an assessment (as one aspect of validity). In the development of graded assessments there seems to have been much concern with criterion or mastery levels, so that the probability of passing is high enough to be encouraging, but clearly not 100 per cent which would make the assessment redundant. In fact, the decision as to cut-off point is ultimately determined by considerations of student motivation, resources and so forth, rather than by some inherent logic of curriculum, pedagogy or the assessment. Hence the 'can do' skill is defined effectively in terms of the characteristics of those students who actually pass the assessment, so that to understand the meaning of 'can do' would require a detailed study of those students and the conditions under which they learnt it.

Which brings us to the issue of context. A study of the draft grade criteria for the GCSE, profile descriptors and the descriptions of levels in many graded assessment schemes shows that almost all do not specify the context in which the assessment is demonstrated. For example, one of the draft grade criteria for English in the domain of writing requires candidates to be able to 'describe a scene or character as the task requires'. There is no localization of the kind of task (perhaps the candidate can do this with some tasks and not with others), nor any attempt to elaborate on what an 'acceptable' description might be.

Such general descriptions follow inevitably from the stated aims of the assessment. Not only would context-specific descriptions be very lengthy, but they would also be impossible to examine exhaustively. Moreover, the more specific the context, the less apparently generalizable the achievement. Since all forms of assessment are inevitably limited to a *sampling* of achievements, a high level of generality is imposed upon the descriptions. This is even more necessary in the GCSE since grade criteria have to be equally applicable to diverse syllabuses in the same subject offered by different examining groups. Yet such general, out-of-context, descriptions can only be valid on the assumption that they relate to demonstrable achievements. Thus we need to assume the existence of a high level competency, such as 'the ability to describe a scene', whose attainment an assessment system is designed to elicit. It is clear, however, that the real existence of such an ability, just like the reality of something called general intelligence, is an assumption, with important consequences. In particular, if the assumption is incorrect, then it is difficult to see what the utility of the description might be.

Suffice it to say that the degree to which achievements are genuinely context-free is very much a matter for debate. There is considerable empirical evidence challenging the notion of context-free assessment (Wolf and Silver, 1986; Nuttall, 1986). It must therefore be of some concern that graded assessments, profile descriptions and the GCSE grade criteria are all predicated on a particular view of the context-independent nature of performance descriptions.

Comparability

We have already referred to the difficulty of finding an 'objective' procedure for ensuring comparability within each form of assessment as well as between them. The experiences of the examining boards in the 1970s is salutary in this respect. They effectively abandoned the search for a foolproof procedure and settled for expert examiner judgement, in addition to a large measure of norm referencing, with all the problems of subjectivity and lack of objective reference which that implies (see Schools Council, 1979; Bardell, Forest and Shoesmith, 1978). In fact such a system resembles a cross between comparability by fiat and comparability on the basis of a strongly shared value-system. An interesting variant is the 'equivalence' between CSE Grade 1 and a GCE O-level 'pass' — an equivalence purely by fiat. No doubt something similar can be put together for the GCSE, although the increased amount of teacher assessment and the differentiated papers will make this more difficult; as a result we may see rather more equivalencing by fiat. An order of magnitude still more difficult is the equivalencing of graded assessments and modular assessment to the GCSE. While it may be possible to specify equivalence by fiat between performance on modules and the GCSE, this will not do for graded assessments in those cases where students are assessed both by graded assessments and by the GCSE. (In other cases, the graded assessments may be accepted as the GCSE assessments.) If an equivalence is established between GCSE grades and levels of the graded assessment in a subject, then it cannot be acceptable for significant proportions of students to pass a graded assessment level and subsequently fail to achieve the equivalent GCSE grade. Yet from all that we know about the unreliability of examinations, it is almost certain that such apparent 'anomalies' will arise. This will expose both the unreliability of the assessments and the impossibility of a consistent one-to-one equivalence. Nor would it be acceptable to eliminate the problem by raising the criteria for the achievement of a given level of the graded assessment, since this will lead to even more students achieving the 'equivalent' GCSE grade but not the graded assessment level than formerly, with a perceived and presumably unacceptable fluctuation in 'standards'. Similarly, if large numbers of students also took separate modular assessments in addition to the GCSE, the same problems would arise. We note that this problem is not a new one in equating; it merely becomes apparent because large numbers of students are exposed to both 'equivalent' forms. It thus represents a major incompatibility which, if not resolved either by decoupling the equivalence or by allowing graded assessments (rigidly controlled by the national criteria) to replace GCSE, will presumably lead to the eventual discrediting of the system and perhaps to the demise of graded assessment.

Usage
There seems to be little discussion and even less evidence about the ways in which the several forms of assessment are to be used in conjunction. To a large extent the equivalencing of graded assessment and modular assessment to GCSE solves the problem (while raising others), but it remains with records of achievement. The Oxford Certificate of Educational Achievement, for example, is planned simply to be an extensive document containing public examination results as well as evidence of other cognitive and non-cognitive achievements. This presentation of detailed information is more likely to be informative than a summary, but in practice it may well be summarized into a single score or grade in different ways before being used, so that its potential utility is negated. The

importance of this can be seen within the GCSE itself where the proposals for grade criteria envisage that separate domain grades will be presented *in addition to* a summary grade over domains. This invites the use of the summary grade as the principal selection device, as occurs at present when employers and higher education selectors simply add up separate grades to form an overall score. When dealing with the more disaggregated information in records of achievement, users may tend to ignore everything other than those things which can easily be summarized into a score or grade or a picking-out of isolated and unreliable pieces of information. Here we see an incompatibility in mode of presentation of results and their likely use which, unless resolved, could lead to a downgrading of much of the information in records of achievement.

Conclusions

We have argued, in a general way, that there are both compatibilities and incompatibilities between the different forms of assessment that will determine the progress of each. We have also argued that the GCSE is the 'prestige' form to which the others are being forced to accommodate and against whose requirements their success will be judged. We have not addressed the intriguing question of whether this needs to be so, nor whether it is the result of contingencies related to sources of funding, the dominance of assessment for selection or other aspects of the educational environment. There is, however, one final issue which we feel, in the long term, is of more importance than the form of the particular kinds of assessment that survive.

All the new forms of assessment have shown at least some concern with objectives and content not previously assessed formally. Thus GCSE has raised the visibility of 'practical' assessment, and records of achievement the visibility of affective characteristics. What has not been questioned, however, is the relative status of different kinds of achievement. Put simply, our present assessment systems embody a hierarchy in which abstract, theoretical achievement is almost always accorded a higher status than the practical and the affective, and this status is intended to reflect what is believed, in the tradition of the 11-plus and 'intelligence', to influence life chances. We find little explicit in the new proposals that presents a real challenge to this view. Thus, while the GCSE pays homage to practical achievement, it is a very puny attempt to rehabilitate the status of practical knowledge and skills, and may readily be subverted. While we are witnessing some substantial changes in the *manner* of doing assessment, we remain sceptical that they will induce any major change in the *aims* of education, and in its fundamental relation to the rest of society. Rather, we can easily envisage a process whereby the flagship of the assessment fleet, the GCSE, actually reinforces those aspects of present public examinations that are concerned with selection, with curriculum control and with the existing status hierarchies of kinds of knowledge.

References

Bardell, G.S., Forrest, G.M. and Shoesmith, D.J. (1978), *Comparability in GCE*. Manchester: JMB on behalf of the GCE Boards.

Broadfoot, P.M., (1979), *Assessment, Schools and Society*, London: Methuen.

Bloom, B.S., Hastings, J.T. and Madaus, G.F. (1971), *Handbook on Formative and Summative Evaluation of Student Learning*. London: McGraw-Hill.

Department of Education and Science (1984), *Records of Achievement: a statement of policy*. London: DES.

_____ (1985), *GCSE: the national criteria*. London: HMSO.

Goldstein, H. (1986), 'Models for equating test scores and for studying the comparability of public examinations' in D.L. Nuttall (ed.), *Assessing Educational Achievement*. Basingstoke, Falmer.

Harrison, A.W. (1982), *Review of Graded Tests*, Schools Council Examinations Bulletin 41. London: Methuen Educationl.

Holland, P. and Rubin, D. (eds.) (1982), *Test Equating*. New York: Academic Press.

Inner London Education Authority (1984), *Improving Secondary Schools* (Hargreaves Report). London: ILEA.

Nuttall, D.L. (1984), 'Doomsday or a new dawn? The prospects of a common system of examining at 16-plus' in P.M. Broadfoot (ed.), *Selection, Certification and Control*. Basingstoke: Falmer.

_____ (1986), 'The validity of assessments', appendix to Wolf and Silver op.cit.

Schools Council (1979), *Standards in Public Examinations: problems and possibilities*. London: Schools Council.

Wolf, A. and Silver, R. (1986), *Work Based Learning: trainee assessment by supervisors*. Sheffield: Manpower Services Commission.